MW01226268

What's Next, Lord?

With Love & Prayer,
Phil. 4/4

Martin E. Ives

Martin

WinePress Publishing
MUKILTEO, WA 98275

Published by:
Winepress Publishing
PO Box 1406
Mukilteo, WA 98275

Cover by **DENHAM**DESIGN, Everett, WA

ISBN: 1-57921-022-8
Library of Congress Catalog Card Number: 97-60627

DEDICATION

To Lois, who loved me for thirty-five years and loved the Lord more. She has gone home before me.

CONTENTS

INTRODUCTION

There is an element of pretend in the use of this book. Pretend that you have never read the Bible before. Try not to jump ahead saying, "This fore-tells Jesus," but receive these increments of revelation by saying, "Wonderful, and what will come next and when?" Allow yourself to see your character in the lives of the people and to see God's character.

Then, in the New Testament we come to Jesus and observe that what had been hinted in the Old Testament is clearly revealed. May you find by this unfolding approach a fresh spiritual exhilaration causing you to burst forth in spontaneous prayer, imaginatively seeing what God had revealed to that time. Revelation from God's mind to man's mind is one of the special elements of the Hebrew-Christian message.

Whether you are a seasoned believer or a sincere seeker, may you also read through the Bible and read this book on appropriate days as a companion book. Many Christians have not read completely through the Bible and would benefit from this discipline. A guide is given at the back of this book.

May you intently consider the steps in God's revelation and then reflect upon yourself as to attitudes and even changes in conduct. Read on! What's next, Lord?

PREFACE

Read this book by itself or as you read through the Bible. In your youth you spent twelve years going through public school. You studied readin', writin' and 'rithmetic twelve times from the simple to more complex. Now suppose that you read through the Bible this year and continue each year for twelve times. What will you have accomplished? The Holy Spirit will have emphasized certain thoughts and heightened your conscience. Your mind will have a good grasp of the organization of the Bible. Many passages will have become favorites, and, likely, you will have memorized some. You will be better prepared to critique your pastor's sermon or teacher's lesson. Critiquing is not cheap criticism. Remember, the Berean Christians looked into the Scriptures (Acts 17:10-11). May this book encourage you to read through the Bible

Reading through the Bible is quite simple, but it needs to be a habit. Plan at least ten minutes each day. When you do this will vary, but maintain the discipline. Enter into reading knowing you are meeting your God—the greatest lover of your soul! Ask the Holy Spirit to help. Don't slow down trying to pronounce names, to know locations, or to remember numbers. Read flowingly.

Alas, some of you will choose to read this book without reading the Bible; and some look at the beehive without reaching in for the honey!

PENTATEUCH

In the beginning God created the heavens and the earth. (Genesis 1:1)

Act I, Scene I: Fellowship
Setting: Darkness, void, no movement.
First character to appear: God.

God wanted something. He willed to create. God spoke and there was response. How did energy and material "listen" to God? We don't know, but they did. God did not delegate his work. He did it himself. He wanted everything a certain way and it was. He was pleased.

As we read through this "new" book, the Bible, let us be open to sense the ability of this God to act and to communicate. If God can create, then surely he can direct people to record what he wants preserved. In the midst of the many gods available in the world, may we be open to the precision and miraculous manner of this God's communication to men and women. This will be a precious fellowship.

We all have some innate sense that there is a God. People crave a God who listens and helps, especially in time of trouble. How much does one need to know about God's character? Do we need to be able to explain God's conduct in scientific terms? Is there any reward for trying to learn about and follow God? Read on and learn of this God from the scenes that follow!

So God created man in his own image, in the image of God he created him; male and female he created them. (Genesis 1:26–27)

What a joy, from the opening chapter of the Bible, that you and I are not in an impersonal world of happenstance. We are here because God wishes to have us. God went ahead of us, prepared a beautiful place for us, and then put us in it. We are here by God's will and love.

"In the image of God" is unique. That is a personal matter and not a material one. We, each man and woman, have some similarity to the character of God. We live with our own quality of love and sense of obedience responding to God's pull of love and will. We have a sense of pleasing or even displeasing God; giving us the ability to respond is so distinct and holy. We are in a Person-to-person life! We may just find this awesome.

People who grow up with a father and mother are often surprised to realize that they have certain personal characteristics of each parent. May we go through this life excited about the characteristics latent within us, which we will soon observe as given by our God—our Creator.

How will we observe? By reading what God is like and what he has done. What will we find? We have high expectations. May we dedicate time each day to reading the Bible and be assured that we will be both humbled and overjoyed at finding the ways we are in God's likeness. What a delicate honor to claim and to act upon every step of one's life!

And I will put enmity between you and the woman, and between your offspring and hers; he will crush your head, and you will strike his heel. (Genesis 3:15)

Act I, Scene II: Broken Fellowship

How well Adam and Eve started in fellowship! They were able to live pleasing to God. When choices were put before them, they chose to disobey God. That is sin. They, and every person since, have found that they cannot live without sinning. What tragedy—broken fellowship! Are you able to admit for your life and say, "I am a person who disobeys"? Adam and Eve were remorseful.

God spoke to Satan. It was not in code but in clarity, "Satan, you will harm a particular Person at some time in the future." But wait, that Person would strike Satan's head, implying that Satan and his work would come to an end. Satan should have cringed, begging for the curse to be undone. (Remember, we are pretending we don't know the New Testament.)

This foretelling of an event is what we call revelation. God announces what he will bring about. This is not what man can arrange.

After the tragedy of disobedience, here is good news for us: The one who coaches us in evil will come to an end! In the meantime, that coach is still influencing our lives today. When will this promise, "crush your head," come about? Later, at God's choice of time. We may conclude that it will not be by a force, but by a person. What kind of person will it be? Surely, God will clearly show us. Trust God. With childlike anticipation, read on and on.

And the Lord God said, "The man has now become like one of us, knowing good and evil. He must not be allowed to reach out his hand and take also from the tree of life and eat, and live forever." (Genesis 3:22)

God had provided so much. All was beautiful and pollution-free in that garden paradise. More important than the physical setting, Adam and Eve's relationship with God had been intimate and the source of joy for living. God gave one restriction—one test. Having failed by eating of the tree of the knowledge of good and evil, they then knew evil by experiencing it. God certainly knows evil, but does not succumb to it. They did, and their close relationship with God was fractured. A very close friend may say, "If you leave me, I'll die," meaning life would be drastically changed by separation. God's statement, "You will surely die," came true as he withdrew his intimacy. It was not death to the body, but to the close relationship.

There was another significant tree. God forcibly put Adam and Eve outside paradise so they would not be able to eat of the tree of life. If they had eaten of it, they would have remained fixed in the condition of alienation from God. By keeping them away from that tree, God kept open the opportunity for healing the broken fellowship at some later time.

Here is good news for all of us: God's plan implies that he would find a way to accomplish reconciliation. Failed—we have. Judged—we are. Pardoned—not yet; but now there is room for that in God's way and time. God is merciful....Next!

I will bless those who bless you, and whoever curses you I will curse; and all peoples on earth will be blessed through you. (Genesis 12:3)

Will Abram be a savior to bring us out of our alienation from God? No, but God did say that Abram would be the means of bringing blessing upon all people. God desires this and we trust him to bring it to pass. If we do not find particular benefits in Abram or his possessions, then we should follow his heirs. Suppose God waits many, many generations. Then we need much patience. Can we still trust God—believe his word when our patience is tested?

What could the lineage of Abram possibly do to benefit all peoples of the earth? There are about five billion of us now. In the lineage, if a banker made an offer, you would expect monetary help; if it were a doctor, you would expect better health. If a judge made an offer, you would hope for a pardon. Ah, there's our greatest need: pardon.

Do you and I allow God to be our judge? Can we claim that our Judge wants all people on earth to be blessed in a manner that he considers truly a blessing? Although at first there appears to be only blessing in the land and goods, read on. Many a generation of the Hebrew people passed without specific answers. We can expect more answers in the course of our reading.

He was priest of God Most High, and he blessed Abram.... Then Abram gave him a tenth of everything. (Genesis 14:18–20)

Abram had engaged in a battle to rescue Lot and had won. The text does not tell us that Abram prayed or worshiped God before going into battle, nor does it mention such afterward. It does say that Abram gave Melchizedek, priest of God Most High, a tenth of everything. He also gave a portion to his men, but he did not keep anything for himself.

What would we have done? Pray and worship maybe, but to give a tenth of all one receives seems like too much! This is the first record of giving that much. Was that a foolish moment for Abram? Not really, for Abram had been gracious shortly before by giving Lot first choice of land. Abram, then, was in character.

We must surely say that Abram showed his gratitude. We often observe a man giving an expensive ring to a certain woman—out of love and gratitude. In our society, we don't think that strange. For Abram, having already been spoken to quite directly by God, giving a tenth was not an inordinate response. Can we offer a tenth to God without knowing if he will respond with an increase in our physical goods? Apparently, whether we offer a tenth or not depends upon the size of our gratitude.

As Melchizedek did not belittle or reject the tithe, apparently giving tithes is a way of pleasing God.

Abram believed the Lord, and he credited it to him as righteousness. (Genesis 15:6)

Abram and Sarai were about to be listed in the "local newspaper" as having one of the longest-standing marriages in town without child. Then God said they would have a son—Abram believed! God said their offspring would be as numerous as the stars—Abram believed!

When God repeated his promise a few years later, the initial reaction of both Abram and Sarai was laughter (Chapters 17–18). Would you have believed had you been Abram or Sarai? Don't be so sure.

What is this new word in the Bible text? Righteousness. Righteousness was to be credited to Abram's sinful personality. On what grounds? Because Abram had generously given God a tithe? No. Abram believed—trusted—that God's word was as good as his Person. Because of that trust, God's assessment of Abram changed from sinful to righteous.

Think for a moment of ourselves. Are we ready for such a pronouncement of righteousness upon ourselves? Or, would we anticipate that such a pronouncement would be as a suit two sizes too small and, hence, uncomfortable. We would have difficulty thanking a person who gave something so uncomfortable. May we, at the least, refrain from our critique of what God bestows until we can learn of what the "suit" is made.

Abram fell face down, and God said to him, "As for me, this is my covenant with you: You will be the father of many nations." (Genesis 17:3–4)

A covenant between God and man. That's rather lop-sided! But that was God's idea, not Abram's. God announced all the benefits and implied there was adequate collateral. He had made a covenant with Noah and one with Abram, regarding land. Now, God changed Abram's name to Abraham: "Father of many." God emphasized that he would be personal with Abraham and the many generations to follow. Surely many nations would require a considerable area. Apparently God would watch over all.

Man's part in the covenant: circumcision. That would be an evident mark in the flesh reminding of God's promise. Specifically, the covenant would be appropriated through a son that Abraham and Sarah would have. Sarai, mother to be, was honored in all of this by her name being changed to Sarah: "Princess."

How would you or I have reacted had we been in Abraham's place? Likely we would have offered several excuses. We need to give praise to Abraham because he believed and proceeded with circumcision.

Have we already seen enough of God's character in this unfolding revelation of himself to accept him at his word? What if he makes succeeding astounding promises? Does God need to give us details of his plans and methods before we can trust? As Abraham and Sarah applied circumcision, they became the examples of believing parents. Always the hard question is: What is my response today?

Now I know that you fear God. (Genesis 22:12)

What a frightening, contradictory, discouraging experience! God had said that Abraham and Sarah would have a son. They did, in spite of old age. He also said the covenant benefiting the following generations would only be through Isaac. In spite of that, Abraham was to sacrifice Isaac! Even Isaac had questions while en route. What was in his father's mind? Surely Abraham prayed as he walked. Would God change his mind and stop them along the way? Would he miraculously bring Isaac back to life? Apparently, Abraham did not shake his fist at God, but proceeded quietly. Surely Abraham was heartbroken, shaking and perspiring as he held the knife above his son!

Many times along a course that seems to be God's will, events occur that appear contradictory. May we pray and proceed without anger. As Abraham picked up the "sticks" and went on until he knew God's final intent, may we go onward through discouraging events until we know God's final direction.

We are so impatient, wanting the answers NOW for a problem. May we allow God to choose the time for revealing daily guidance and for unfolding the salvation plan. Maybe, in the midst of our awkward moments, we can hear the words, "Now I know that you fear God."

God has revealed that listening and obeying are pleasing to him. But what a test. Will there be another?

I said, "O Lord, God of my master Abraham, if you will, please grant success to the journey on which I have come" (Genesis 24:42). *I bowed down and worshiped the Lord. I praised the Lord, the God of my master Abraham, who had led me."* (Genesis 24:48)

How astounding that this God, who shapes the earth and changes nations, chooses to be attentive to a servant seeking a wife for his master! Abraham had the attitude that God would have something to do with this matter, so he commissioned his servant on oath. Abraham believed an angel would guide. Notice that Abraham wanted the wife for his son Isaac to be of similar background and a believer in the same God.

Note that the servant was a believer and was fervent in prayer. He gave God a suggestion, not a requirement, for how to identify the right woman. When that much of his prayer had clearly been answered, he gave God the credit by bowing and worshiping: "Praise be to the Lord, the God of my master Abraham, who has not abandoned his kindness and faithfulness to my master. As for me, the Lord has led me" (vs.27).

The servant testified that God had answered his prayer when he met Rebekah's family. Again, upon arriving home and meeting Isaac in a field, he told of God's guidance. Do you and I tell others of God's tender workings in life? This reveals some of God's personal character. What's next?

Then Jacob made a vow, saying, "If God will be with me and will watch over me on this journey I am taking and will give me food to eat and clothes to wear so that I return safely....Then the Lord will be my God....I will give you a tenth." (Genesis 28:20–22)

Jacob surely heard his father, Isaac, recount numerous times how Grandfather Abraham had sent the servant to choose a wife for Isaac. Those prayers were answered. Now Isaac prayerfully sends Jacob for a wife.

En route, Jacob had a vision of angels attending him and a message from God Himself. His message was throbbing with assurance, "I will give you....I am with you and will watch over you....I will bring you back....I will not leave you...."

"If Granddad will take me fishing, of course I'll go!" Only this was not Granddad but God making promises. Jacob immediately made a worship place and responded with his vow that God would indeed be his God. Jacob would even give a tenth of his assets to God.

All of this was farther reaching than the immediate goal of finding a wife. God used the occasion to reveal his personal watchfulness over daily living. Perhaps God gave you assurance in Sunday morning worship or while driving and listening to a Christian radio station. Have you allowed that assurance to remain clear in your mind and heart so as to guide you in daily living? Can you be as resolute: "I will..."?

Am I in the place of God?...God intended it for good. (Genesis 50:19–20)

Joseph could have been shaking his fist at God during those earlier years. Sold by his brothers—what wretched cruelty! Joseph could have cursed God when he was thrown into prison because of the wrong accusation by a woman. God tested Joseph's character—Joseph shined. He gave God credit for interpreting dreams and for guiding him in his responsibilities. Maybe, being human, he was rather angry at his brothers and was willing to stay away from his family until he could return in a way pleasing to God.

But his brothers came to him in Egypt. He tested them, letting them come to some grief. With hints and then with clarity, he revealed himself to his brothers. Finally, all the family came to live in Egypt under Joseph's protection.

However, when his father, Jacob, died how would Joseph act toward his brothers? This, also, was a test. "Don't be afraid. Am I in the place of God?" Joseph shines again! Did you ever have the opportunity for revenge...and not carry it out?

In addition: "God intended it for good...." Before Joseph could see how 2 plus 2 would make 4, he trusted that God was carrying out a plan for good. Upon his deathbed, Joseph repeated what he undoubtedly heard from his father: God intended to return the people to the promised land (Chp. 46). Can you be patient in adversity? Can you handle little or much? Do you believe God is sovereign over events?

When the Lord saw that he had gone over to look, God called to him from within the bush, "Moses, Moses!" And Moses said, "Here I am." (Exodus 3:4)

(We skip over some 400 years from Joseph to Moses' life centering in Egypt [Exodus 12:40].)

When we see a spectacle, we can stand back and say, "Ahhh," or go nearer and inquire. Moses did the latter. He was brave, not only because the bush was burning, but because he might meet a challenge. He did, as we will see. This was not a moment of common grace—looking at a sunrise or sunset—it was a holy moment. The angel, speaking for God, quickly indicated familiarity with Moses and his people. This was comforting.

Further assurance for Moses was that this One was the God of his father, of Abraham, of Isaac and of Jacob. Evidently those great leaders were alive! They had died bodily deaths but were alive in God's presence. Wonderful.

Can you or I experience special moments with God without trying to rationalize as to the "how" and be patient about the "why"? Moses did not mutter or turn eloquent but reacted by humbly hiding his face. Inside, he must have wondered and perhaps been a little afraid of what would be said next.

Often with assurances, come challenges. Will God challenge Moses? Let's look further at the next paragraphs.

*God said to Moses, "I AM who I AM. This is what you are
to say to the Israelites: 'I AM has sent me to you.'" God also
said to Moses, "Say to the Israelites, 'The Lord, the God of
your fathers—the God of Abraham, the God of Isaac and the
God of Jacob—has sent me to you.' This is my name forever."*
(Exodus 3:14–15)

Amazing! God IS. This God who created this world and
universe, the creatures and people, continues to exist. God
wills them to be. Moses was to present that concept to the
Israelites. This definition would encourage them in future
difficulties. Moses, too, needed encouragement, for he
envisioned problems.

An old song has the challenge: "Got any mountains you
cannot tunnel through?…" God gives encouragement in
the midst of difficulty by the reassurance that he consistently exists. Cling to this. God is; HE IS!

Further, God is God of the three great statesmen—
Abraham, Isaac and Jacob. There is no comfort in hearing
of some god who is over dead things. God was announcing
for the second time that these three yet live. There is life
after this earthly life! This is as sure as God's character,
and his character is described by his name. His name and
his character are constant.

Listen and learn from God. Be ready to live with God
forever. God wants us. Are you apprehensive? Remember
that he made us with some likeness to himself so that being with God would seem appropriate at some time in the
future. There is more help and further truth to be made
known as we read on in the Bible!

But when the magicians tried to produce gnats by their secret arts, they could not....The magicians said to Pharaoh, "This is the finger of God." (Exodus 8:18–19)

Knockout in the fourth round! The magicians matched God, point for point, for three rounds: Change a staff into a snake—they did; turn water into blood—they did; bring frogs—they did, produce gnats—they did...NOT! It was time to tell Pharaoh that they were out of the game. We see that it was God's strong arm alone from there on.

What was the purpose of the contest as God announced it? It was "that you may know there is no one like the Lord our God" (vs.10). Why did God need to go through such a battery of contests? The simple answer seems to be that man often looks around for another god; even considering himself, as did Pharaoh. But this God is the one who made the earth and people. He continues in relationships with people, especially directing this group, the Israelites.

These plagues were such destruction upon people, animals, and land. You, O man, so easily turn to your ideas of a god. Can you accept that there is one God who is revealing himself; trying to arrest you and hold you in his loving custody while he explains matters of the future?

By day the Lord went ahead of them in a pillar of cloud to guide them on their way and by night in a pillar of fire to give them light, so that they could travel by day or night. Neither the pillar of cloud...nor the pillar of fire...left its place in front of the people (Exodus 13:21–22). *Throughout the night the cloud brought darkness to the one side and light to the other side; so neither went near the other.* (Exodus 14:20)

See God. See what God can do. Sometimes we need to be childlike and see what God can do. The motion picture and TV presentations of the Exodus help us feel the emotions. Courage was mixed with fear; looking forward included looking back.

God directed these people and inanimate things for his purpose, "Turn back,...Raise your staff and stretch out your hand over the sea...." He moved the angel and the pillar of cloud to the rear, and divided the water. God wrenched strength, courage and safety away from the Egyptians by hardening Pharaoh's heart and destroying the army.

What is the lesson? "The Egyptians will know that I am the Lord when I gain glory through Pharaoh...." Moses announced that the Lord would fight for his people. At the end of the event, they "saw the great power the Lord displayed...feared the Lord and put their trust in him and in Moses...." Are you trusting this God? Have you come far enough that you can tell someone you are trying to trust God?

That evening quail came and covered the camp, and in the morning there was a layer of dew around the camp. When the dew was gone, thin flakes like frost on the ground appeared on the desert floor. (Exodus 16:13–14)

A million people—more or less—were to be fed! No transport trucks from the grocery stores; no emergency helicopter drops. God brought the food. He flew the quail into camp and distributed the bread on the ground. Did anyone drop to their knees? Did anyone have tears on their cheeks? Perhaps a few; the record doesn't tell us. Those who grumble don't respond with gratitude but do frequently vocalize their complaints.

They had just seen God's strong arm overcome the Egyptians. Now they saw that God would not leave them or forsake them. God had met their needs and their wants. God had even said he would protect them from the diseases of the Egyptians (15:26). What more could one want of his God?

How could the people ever—ever—ever turn aside and look for another god? Would I have been content with this God who had proved himself if I had lived then?

Does God care if we include other gods in our lives? God speaks to that as a most serious issue in the next revelation.

You shall have no other gods before me. You shall not make for yourself an idol....You shall not misuse the name of the Lord your God....Remember the Sabbath day....Honor your father and your mother....You shall not murder. You shall not commit adultery. You shall not steal....You shall not give false testimony....You shall not covet. (Exodus 20:3–17)

If the Israelites followed these guides, they would please God. He reveals not only some of his character, but also what character he would like of us.

Wouldn't it be wonderful if God would clearly guide you throughout the day with such as the pillar and the cloud of which we just read a few pages earlier? A parent places his hand on the back of a young child to guide through a crowd. For an older child, a parent sends him alone with a few verbal instructions. Although God had just guided the people by physical means, now he gives a succinct but very clear list of verbal instructions. Can we admit that we often need to be told? We don't always please God automatically.

Some people are resentful of God using the "don't do this" method. "It's so childish," they say. We used that method with our children and that was in preparation for maturity. Trust God that this is an adult relationship for guiding our lives in spiritual maturity.

This guidance starts with "no other gods!" God certainly indicates that he is exclusive.

See, I am sending an angel ahead of you to guard you along the way and to bring you to the place I have prepared. (Exodus 23:20)

An Angel! That's better than a detailed map and road signs. The angel guarded along the way and brought them to their destination. Surely, if we had been there, we would have reveled in that announcement. Guarding was needed, for the mass of people and animals was certainly vulnerable to attack by marauders, heat and lack of water. Direction was needed, for it had been nearly five centuries since Abraham traveled through the land promised to his offspring. Just how often did the angel speak or point the way? We don't know. We know that the arrangement was adequate.

What would our reaction have been had God said to us that he would be an enemy to our enemies, bless our food and water, take away sickness, give a full life span, send a terror ahead, drive out the enemies, and establish the borders? Would we have been excited primarily about these provisions for physical security? These are words given after pages of instruction of responsibility on how to live regarding personal conduct. It seems so easy to change the subject from personal responsibility, "What *I* am to do," to, "What *God* is going to do for me."

God, thank you for angels, but help us to listen closely to your words that tell us clearly how to conduct our lives pleasing to you.

For the life of the creature is in the blood, and I have given it to you to make atonement for yourselves on the altar; it is the blood that makes atonement for one's life. (Leviticus 17:11)

As I read on, I come to a bloody part; the instruction is to kill the animal and display the blood. Some people are critical of God regarding this. The hunter and the farmer kill animals in order to have the benefit of sustaining human life. The benefit of which God speaks is not helping physical living by eating; rather, helping one's relationship with God by giving something of worth. The animal was worth much as part of the shepherd's assets. It was "wasted"—sacrificed. God is worth it even if there was no benefit to us.

But there is benefit to us: atonement. Atonement is a hiding or covering of something; in this case, sin. Also, there is the reestablishment of a personal relationship with God. Sometimes a little gift to a friend helps break resentment, and the friendship is then open again. What a delight that God accepts us close to Himself. That is at-one-ment—atonement!

Had we been there, we might have said to God, "God, what good is this animal which is so beneath our dignity?"

God might have replied, "Son and daughter, just wait and I'll show you a far greater sacrifice later. Use this for now." May we wait patiently for his plan to be revealed step by step.

But if you will not listen to me and carry out all these commands....Then I will... (Leviticus 26:14–18, 27)

In a most frightening way, God has our attention, "If you will not listen"—three times!

First of all, a relationship with God includes an honesty that we might disobey. We have trouble admitting that to ourselves. We excuse ourselves for disobeying, "See, it didn't affect my family or job," or "Others in the church are doing that." Any covenant includes conditional clauses like, "But if...." Yes, God knows well that we do need to be told there are consequences for breaking a covenant with him.

This may be a good time to ask: What is the purpose of this life on earth. Is it to live many, many years? Is it to have health until the day of death? Is it to have many assets of money or things? Had we been there at the time God announced all of his instructions, his benefits and his warnings, what would have been our conclusion? Our purpose on earth seems to be to love God so much that we want to obey him. Doing that, we will also benefit greatly now in this life.

Secondly, as we read of God's relationship, we find that God is so patient. Surely we find illustrations of that in our own lives. Isn't God's tug of love humbling and at the same time a building of self-worth? Aren't you glad God did not make us robots?

Because you did not trust in me enough to honor me as holy...you will not bring this community into the land I give them. (Numbers 20:12)

True, God told Moses to speak to the rock. True, Moses struck the rock. Water gushed out! "Isn't that all right, God?"

"NO!"

"But God, Moses obeyed and lead the people for several years, even out of Egypt. But God, Moses even pled for the people, 'Forgive their sin—but if not, then blot me out of the book' (Exodus 32:32). God, you spoke to him as a friend (Exodus 33:11). For one disobedience, this pronouncement seems so harsh."

Moses violated only part of God's command; God announced that Moses would not lead the people into the promised land. I am deeply humbled.

Moses' act of disobedience was in public. What if we reviewed all of our thoughts and acts done in private?

What position of responsibility do you have? In what way do you water down and modify God's commands as you stand before other people? Sure, Moses was getting old and would need to resign his leadership some day and die. That's not the point. What daily honor of the Lord do you and I give before other people who watch us? Is there a day off? No. Honor of God does not take a holiday.

God is stern. Are you humbled?

The Lord said to Moses, "Make a snake and put it up on a pole; anyone who is bitten can look at it and live." So Moses made a bronze snake and put it up on a pole. Then when anyone was bitten by a snake and looked at the bronze snake, he lived. (Numbers 21:8–9)

The people impatiently grumbled against Moses and God how many times now? This time they mentioned lack of bread and water; indeed, significant items. How many times have we grumbled and spoken to God about things that seemed important? Do we use money to try to buy our way out of a predicament? Perhaps God would like us to develop patience.

Can we ask God for help in living with an existing predicament? Instead of being so quick to ask for removal of a problem, ask for patience in the midst of it. If we become cheerful on the job or in the home, we may be the means of changing a predicament.

Yet, also we need to look to God for a special solution of his arrangement. God did not remove the snakes at first, but told Moses to make a bronze snake. Those who were bitten and looked at it lived. Would we have looked? Anyone from across the populace could look at the snake held high. Anyone! Only belief or trust was required.

God announced this unique solution. Would anything like this occur again? Next.

What other nation is so great as to have their gods near them the way the Lord our God is near us whenever we pray to him? And what other nation is so great as to have such righteous decrees and laws as this body of laws I am setting before you today? (Deuteronomy 4:7–8, 32-40)

What praise Moses gave of God! What acknowledgment he gave as to the foundation of the nation Israel. During Moses' life a new nation came into being, distinctly different from those around it, and he took time to thank God.

Are we convinced that enormous influences are brought about by this God-above-all-gods? Do we desire that this God have a similar close relationship with us today? Thus far through the Bible, we have been told of the beginning of human life, the beginning of sin, that God offers a means of atonement (Leviticus 17:11), and that he loves and gives benefits to those who endeavor to trust him. There is none like Him!

The Hebrew word most frequently used for God is a somewhat common word for deity. Have you ever heard a friend tell you about someone named Tom? Suddenly you concluded that he was the Tom you knew. Thus far, you are presented with true stories about God, and suddenly you realize he is THE GOD. -

What should we do? Reread verses 39–40. He is in heaven and, at the same time, on earth! Acknowledge him and keep his decrees. Note: "It will go well with you and your children."

CONVERSATIONAL PRAYER

Now we have read the first five books of the Bible. We understand that Moses wrote those books. Together, they are called the *Law*, the *Law of Moses*, or the *Pentateuch*. Let's summarize and enthusiastically express some of what God, step by step, has revealed of himself and of what he wants of us. Using a first-person, conversational style in this prayer allows that things are not necessarily in logical order. Each one of us would say things differently from the other.

God, thank you for telling me a little about your creating the world and for wanting me to have a life-visit on this earth. You can arrange things and people so well. I don't resent that; I call that being sovereign. Yet, you told people they are responsible to live certain ways or they would suffer consequences. Somehow you choose to love human life. You seem to crave a closeness even with me. I want that, yet I'm afraid. I'm fickle—you're patient. Time and again you invite. Time and again you forgive. I'm trying to listen and to obey what you have revealed. You open your thoughts a little at a time. You show enough of yourself to tell me you are special, the only One. You show that you want to help overcome enemies. My worst enemy tends to be a wrong lifestyle I so easily slip into. Please steer my life. Thank you, God, that you want to put a bandage over my sin spots. Do you have a righteous kiss for my hurts that's better than my mother's kiss? I want to read all of the Bible and learn so much more about you and about myself. Thank you, God. Thank you.

(May you pray, incorporating promises and assurances you have just read. Express yourself using your own vocabulary, not imitating others.)

HISTORICAL

And as soon as the priests...set foot in the Jordan, the water flowing downstream will be cut off... (Joshua 3:9–13). *Then the Lord said, "...Have all the people give a loud shout; then the wall of the city will collapse...."* (6:2–5).

God bid that the priests step into the flooding Jordan River. As their feet touched the edge, the river stopped flowing! Later, the Israelites marched around Jericho as directed. Upon trumpeting and shouting, the walls fell! Those fallen walls have been found by archeologists.

Had you been one of those priests, would you have snickered in disbelief as you put your foot in the river? Had you walked around Jericho six times, would you have been thinking of hurrying back to the tent to eat?

The Israelites could have waited until after the flood stage and then forded the river. Likely, in due time, they could have captured Jericho by human battle. Why did God direct them in these special ways? "He did this so that all the peoples of the earth might know that the hand of the Lord is powerful and so that you might always fear the Lord your God" (4:24).

God, I don't need to know how you did those things. I do need to remember that you did them then, and I expect you to do special things in my life now. As they were to tell others "what these stones mean" (4:1–7), may I be faithful in telling of the special events in my life.

Gideon replied, "...Why has all this happened to us?...How can I save Israel?...Give me a sign....Dew only on the fleece....Ground covered with dew." (Judges 6)

It is so easy for us today to point our finger at Gideon and say, "You chicken," for asking for so many reassurances. Yet, as hesitant as he was initially, he built an altar to God and tore down the altar of Baal. He started off with an army, only to be told to reduce it. What...only three hundred? He complied and won the battle.

Apparently, one does not need to know the answers of how, why and when. One needs to get down off the human-intellect-is-god stool and kneel before God. God can, and often does, choose leaders. Some of those chosen are not the ones a personnel committee from the local government or from the church would have picked. The result of the leadership of Gideon: "The land enjoyed peace forty years" (8:28).

What happened after Gideon died? "The Israelites again prostituted themselves to the Baals...and did not remember the Lord their God." (8:33–34) How sad! Trouble soon broke out. Have we learned our lesson from this? Worship the God who created and directs this world and there will be benefits in life. Forget God, and there will be more than the usual troubles.

But they forgot the Lord their God....They cried out to the Lord and said, "We have sinned...." Then the Lord...delivered you.... (1 Samuel 12:9–11)

Samuel, in his farewell speech to all of Israel, reviewed evidences of God's work from Egypt onward. This was a scenario: they forgot God, cried for help, admitted sin, and he delivered them. How sad that they forgot God, and yet this seems so human. Yes, we have forgotten God at times, too. Can each of us admit that for ourselves?

What happens when you forget? Have you ever gone to the store and forgotten your money? The consequence is at least being embarrassed. Have you let your mind wander for a moment while driving and come close to having a serious accident? With a little perspiration, you can envision the near calamity with a pedestrian or with another vehicle. When you forget God and go on your willful way, can you foresee the consequence?

Call to God, not just for help, but to say, "I have sinned." Those seem to be sweet words, likened to a beautiful aroma wafting upward to God.

Did God forget the people? No, nor does he forget *you*. Isn't that beautiful! Even though you grieve God, that does not cut the line of communication. He hears you, he forgives you, he delivers you—time and again. Deserving? No, yet he forgives you. Cling to this God! Who else?

*O Sovereign Lord!...And who is like your people Israel—
the one nation on earth that God went out to redeem as a people
for himself, and to make a name for himself,...so that your
name will be great forever.* (2 Samuel 7:18–29)

David mentioned several times in this prayer that God
is sovereign. He was humble, saying, "Who am I, O Sovereign Lord?" Even as he spoke highly of the nation Israel,
David said God's purpose was "to make a name for Himself."

God is not a servant. Then, we are not to say to God,
"Give me this and do that for me." Whether or not our
names and positions are prominent in society is not the
point. What God does to us, through us and for us is for His
name's sake.

We should do as David and give a testimony. Have you
told friends of your thankfulness to God for your life and
family? Have you told of circumstances in which God
worked that were above what you could have expected by
human effort and arrangement?

"O Sovereign Lord!" He is the important one. We are
subservient, yet, we have a very significant worth in life
because of that very relationship to God. This is well expressed by the Westminster Shorter Catechism (mid-17th
century): "What is the chief end of man?...Man's chief end
is to glorify God, and to enjoy him forever." That gives excitement to life!

The Lord is my rock, my fortress and my deliverer; my God is my rock, in whom I take refuge, my shield and the horn of my salvation. (2 Samuel 22:2–3)

David had gone through good and bad times in life: He had killed Goliath, he won acclaim in battles, and he married into the king's family. King Saul harassed him for years. David spared Saul's life more than once before he became king. One son rebelled against him and then was killed. He sinned with Bathsheba and murdered Uriah. Yet, as a whole, he was a righteous man.

Apparently, it was near the end of his kingship that David acclaims God as his Rock, Fortress, Deliverer and Salvation. In his human life he was so thankful for security from enemies. In addition, he seemed to claim freedom from all that is binding of this earthly life; that is confidence in eternity. In the meantime, he declared that God had dealt fairly with him.

"As for God, his way is perfect; the word of the Lord is flawless. He is a shield for all who take refuge in him. For who is God besides the Lord? And who is the Rock except our God?...The Lord lives! Praise be to my Rock! Exalted be God, the Rock, my Savior!" (vs.31–32, 47).

I, too, want to worship this God. Next.

So be strong, show yourself a man, and observe what the Lord your God requires: Walk in his ways, and keep his decrees and commands, his laws and requirements,...so that you may prosper in all you do and wherever you go. (1 Kings 2:2–3)

David spoke to his son, Solomon, in a beautiful, fatherly way—encouraging and firm—near the time of his death. He did not say he was perfect, but emphasized his close relationship with God. David could say that, for his life had shown it.

And you, fathers and mothers, how much can you say to your sons or daughters about your life with God and still be credible? Are there some changes you should make? David was a shepherd, musician, hymn writer, soldier, general, dependable friend, forgiver of enemies, sinner, worshiper, and both tender and disciplined. You likely will not be known for that many abilities and qualities. Are you known primarily for your praise of God and also some measure of obedience to God's directives?

David also indicated a benefit, "So that you may prosper in all you do and wherever you go." Anyone who comes to God for the purpose of prospering is selfish. Anyone coming to God in close fellowship for his sake will indeed find corollary blessings. Let us use God's standards, remembering that we are made in his image. David lived an exciting life with what he knew of God. Do You?

So give your servant a discerning heart to govern your people and to distinguish between right and wrong. For who is able to govern this great people of yours? (1 Kings 3:9)

God made an offer to Solomon, "Ask for whatever you want me to give you." Look at Solomon's answer: He was thankful for the way God had treated his father David, was humble in that God had allowed him to be the heir, and was humble about his ability to perform his duties over such a vast multitude. That was indeed the great problem—the multitude; and he asked for great wisdom.

God was pleased that he did not ask selfishly for long life, wealth or death of enemies. He gave assurance that he would give to Solomon what he asked, and also riches, honor and long life in addition! Solomon was to live in obedience. He returned to Jerusalem and dedicated himself in worship to God.

Will such an offer ever be issued again by God? At this point, let us receive this as an illustration of God's love and attention. A youngster is so pleased that Grandfather took him to the fair that he does not try to calculate whether Grandfather will ever do it again. He simply accepts the trip to the fair as characteristic of a grandfather's love. Let us worship God and live in obedience, ready for whatever God offers us out of his great love. Next...

To have a temple built for my name...temple for the name of the Lord, the God of Israel. ...'My name shall be there'... ...so that all the people of the earth may know that the Lord is God and that there is no other. (1 Kings 8)

The NAME. Not John, not Jane, but the NAME. Not *a* god. Play the holy record over again: the God who created, who judged many times, who rescued numerous times, who directed redemption through a sacrifice, who built this immense nation—THAT God! There is no substitute. There is no facsimile. There is no twin. There is no clone. There were gods in the next-door nations. They had not the NAME.

God came and "the glory of the Lord filled his temple." His presence was obvious. His presence was real. His presence was awesome.

Today, at the side of your church building, there is a sign that indicates your church is a little different from others down the street. However, when you enter for worship, is it obvious the NAME is there? Does the worship lift up that same NAME and humble the people before the NAME? "Hallowed be your NAME!"

If you are not in the habit of going to a church, try one that will help you become convicted that "the Lord is God and that there is no other." Hallelujah!

[Elijah] "If the Lord is God, follow Him; but if Baal is god, follow him…the God who answers by fire—he is God.…" [The people] "The Lord, he is God! The Lord—he is God! (1 Kings 18:16–39)

A most dramatic portion of the Bible! Many actors or opera singers could take an hour to portray all this on stage. Let's cut through the drama.

Purpose: to remind the people that God is truly God. Method: a contest between Elijah and the prophets of Baal; or really, between God and Baal. (Can you hear Elijah taunting?) Result: the people saw God dramatically present himself in power.

How fickle the people were. True, they of Israel had several kings who led them away from God and to Baal. Is that an excuse for forgetting what God had done in the past? If you experience the disheartening loss of your job, do you look for another god? If a loved one dies, do you look for another god? Does it really take a dramatic miracle to maintain your trust in God? Will you choose to trust God even when a "friend" continues to pressure you to turn away?

Does what you have learned thus far about God by reading the Bible help you to recognize what God has done in your life? May you trust him for tomorrow without any fickleness or turning away.

Elisha sent a messenger to say to him, "Go, wash yourself seven times in the Jordan, and your flesh will be restored and you will be cleansed." (2 Kings 5:10)

Another dramatic moment which actors and opera singers would enjoy. General Naaman was a high Syrian official. He had leprosy, a progressively destructive disease. He was so desperate that he listened to the advice of his young maid even though she was a Hebrew. He traveled afar bringing a letter from his king to Elisha's king. Fortunately, Elisha heard about the letter and sent for General Naaman.

Not many people tell a general what to do. Elisha had the audacity to send his messenger instead of stepping outside himself and, furthermore, to tell the general to step into the muddy Jordan River to wash seven times! General Naaman turned away in a rage. Can you hear his raving? Finally, upon the pleading of his servants, he condescended to dip into the Jordan once, twice, even seven times. His flesh was whole and youthful. "Now I know that there is no God in all the world except in Israel."

Are you inclined to argue, saying, "I would not do it that way, God"? Such a statement is reprehensible when we put it in words, but don't we often think that way? This is precisely a hard lesson for each of us to learn: God is God; he sets the boundaries for life.

Leprosy was often used as a symbol of being spiritually unclean. Are you desirous of being clean physically and spiritually for the company of your friends, and especially for company with God?

49

Neither before nor after Josiah was there a king like him who turned to the Lord as he did—with all his heart and with all his soul and with all his strength, in accordance with all the law of Moses. (2 Kings 23:25)

Josiah was a youngster when he became king. He pleased God and arranged for repair of the Temple. The Book of the Law, or the Book of the Covenant—the first five books of our Bible, was found. He read in Genesis, Chapter 9, of the covenant that God made with Noah, that God will not again use a flood to destroy life on the earth. Further, Chapter 15 gives God's promise of the land to Abraham and his descendants, including God's presence and care for his people. Josiah read to the people, the least and the greatest. He vowed to be obedient in action, heart and soul, and the people followed by pledging themselves. The King cleansed the Temple physically and morally, killing the priests of the cults. He arranged a memorable Passover for the people, thus renewing their part of the covenant.

You and I find life so difficult to keep on an even keel. Have you ever watched the helmsman of a large ship? He constantly makes adjustments in direction by small and large movements of the wheel. From Josiah's example, may we strive for a straight course in life following this same God with heart and soul and strength. God keeps his part of the covenant.

Praise be to the Lord....There is no God like you in heaven or on earth—you who keep your covenant of love with your servants who continue wholeheartedly in your way....Will God really dwell on earth with men?...Hear from heaven, your dwelling place; and when you hear, forgive....Confess your name and turn from their sin....And forgive your people.... (2 Chronicles 6)

Solomon adored God, made a confession of sin, gave thanksgiving and included supplication. Here is an excellent outline for prayer: A-C-T-S.

A: Adoration. Can you give praise to God for who He is, even if there appears to be no benefit to you? Some people call upon God only to elicit personal gain. Think instead of the majesty of God.

C: Then, surely there comes to your mind some need for confession. Having contrasted yourself with God, not fellow man, give humble confession.

T: Thanksgiving follows. Please don't sit back and say (or sing), "If I were a rich man..." Express thanks for things and especially for relationships you now have. "Count your many blessings...."

S: To supplicate is to ask earnestly and humbly. Solomon appealed to God, true; but mainly on behalf of the people.

How do you pray? Try all of the above.

And who knows but that you have come to royal position for such a time as this? (Esther 4:14)

Esther, a Jewish woman, becomes queen by an unusual set of circumstances. Now, Haman cleverly plots against the entire Jewish populace. Can you see the actors moving about the stage? Mordecai, Esther's uncle, urges Esther to use her position to save her people. That may be the very reason God had her chosen as queen! But that was real life, a very serious predicament.

She could sit, weep and wring her hands, or raise both arms and shake both fists at God. She could barge in upon the king and possibly lose her life. Instead, she asked all the Jews to fast with her. Likely, that included prayer.

What do you do in response to a dilemma? You can wring your hands, shake your fists or barge ahead. You may lose the opportunity or your job. Or, you can speak to Christian friends and ask them to join you in prayer. On the third day, Esther started to carry out a plan. She was even willing that she lose her position. Do you tell God when and how to solve a problem? Do you say, "Anything, God, but don't endanger me?" That was not Esther's response.

God saved the Jews. However, there was also a very special outcome, "And many people of other nationalities became Jews because fear of the Jews had seized them" (8:17). Can you tell your friends of being directed in a dilemma so that they may take a better look at this God?

CONVERSATIONAL PRAYER

Now we have read twelve more books of the Bible—Joshua through Esther. These are called the Historical Books. What highlights and fresh applications come to mind for your life? Here is one person's prayer. Using a first-person, informal style allows that these thoughts are not necessarily in a logical order.

God, thank you for letting me point my finger at others and then gradually seeing that so much of their character is in me as well. I don't like my spouse or friend telling me how weak I am, but I can accept criticism from you. You are amazing, God, as you work through human leaders and arrange nations. If I can trust the chairlift to take me to the mountain peak, why can't I trust you more consistently? You gave us commands as rules for the road of life. I seem to bring upon myself so many problems by not steering my life in obedience to those commands. Oh yes, the hymn says: "Trust and obey, for there's no other way...." I'll keep trying. You do forgive me so often, thank you. I don't want to waver back and forth as though I think I need some special event to reconvince me of your worth and truth. Also, I'll try not to say, "God, your ways are not the best." That's a way of pretending that I am a god. How do I dare do that? Yes, I know I have a sinful nature and what comes out merely indicates what is within. I'll try to follow you with my heart, soul and strength and to seek things that uphold your name rather than mine. I'm glad that when this life is finished, I will enter into your eternal life without all this present wavering.

(May you pray, incorporating promises and assurances you have just read. Express yourself using your own words.)

POETICAL

Naked I came from my mother's womb, and naked I will depart. The Lord gave and the Lord has taken away; may the name of the Lord be praised. (Job 1:21)

Job had just lost his assets by theft and his sons and daughters by natural disaster. If this happened to you, what would your reaction be? Would you shake your fist at God, or withdraw and wallow in self-pity? Job "did not sin by charging God with wrongdoing." Then, God allowed Satan to strike Job's health, but not to take his life. Satan had enormous power, yet was limited by God.

Job's wife had more difficulty in all this, "Curse God and die!"

Job responded, "Shall we accept good from God, and not trouble?" In the midst of great mental and physical suffering, Job cursed the day of his birth and struggled in conversation with his four friends.

What things have you said when you were not certain of your life? Recently, a woman entered a hospital with a serious heart condition and, the next day, her husband suddenly died on the way home from his doctor's appointment. She was angry at God, very angry. Can you accept that God sometimes allows difficulties in life that you cannot explain? Ask God all the questions you want. He likely won't answer them. Can you be patient even if your neighbor taunts you saying, "Where is your God?" Can you come to the conclusion with Job that God is great, even if mysterious?

Dare we ask what is next?

I know that my Redeemer lives, and that in the end he will stand upon the earth. And after my skin has been destroyed, yet in my flesh I will see God....How my heart yearns within me! (Job 19:25–27)

Job, is it a beautiful sunset that inspires you to write? No, God gave him moments of inspiration. Job, are you pretending that you are not in pain; that sickness is not real? No, for he had just said, "Have pity on me," and earlier said he wished he had not been born. He never denied what was happening to him. Pain and sorrow were real.

All right, let's listen to Job. His Redeemer lives. Job admits he needs a redeemer, even apart from his sickness. His regular custom was to give sacrifices for his children (1:5). He had spoken of an advocate and intercessor (16:19–20). Apparently, Job believed in a person separate from God who would properly represent God. This Redeemer would stand on the earth. That is not one floating among the trees or hovering in a corner of the house. It seems to be one who is physical enough to be approachable. Job is certain that after his body deteriorates, he will experience God with some kind of new body. He, for himself, will see God. How his heart yearns for those future experiences.

How and when, Lord?

I am unworthy—how can I reply to you? I put my hand over my mouth. I spoke once, but I have no answer—twice, but I will say no more (Job 40:4–5). I know that you can do all things; no plan of yours can be thwarted. You asked, "Who is this that obscures my counsel without knowledge?" Surely I spoke of things I did not understand, things too wonderful for me to know (Job 42:2–3).

Between these two quotations is given a grand contrast of persons, a contrast between God and Job. It's so easy to try pushing God into a mold instead of understanding that God may well be different than our imagining. When we expect answers to all our questions, we are trying to make God accountable to ourselves. That's wrong. Many adverse incidents of life are inexplicable according to our limited view of God. May we step down from the pinnacle of pride to the wholesomeness of humility as did Job; admit that God is too wonderful to explain.

Later, God "made him prosperous again and gave him twice as much as he had before." Why? We don't know. Most people never ask the question, "Why do I have prosperity?" The ungodly people do not taunt us with that question. Yet that is just as difficult to answer as the questions about adversity. Please, let God be Himself—Sovereign!

The kings of the earth take their stand and the rulers gather together against the Lord and against his Anointed One. (Psalm 2:2)

Remember that in Genesis we were told that a special Person would come and defeat Satan. Now there is mention of a special Person as God's Anointed One. This One will at some time be installed on Mount Zion as King, such as no human being has ever been king. He will be the Son and God will be the Father in such a relationship as has never been seen before (vs.7). How can that be? God often does not explain, he simply announces. The phrases "serve the Lord" and "kiss the Son" imply high character and even equality with God. Are there two Gods? Yet, throughout the Scripture we have been learning that there is only One.

This Anointed One to come will evidently have a visible, physical body. People of nations across the earth are offered a relationship. Some will favor and some will oppose this One. There is awesome responsibility for those of both opinions. God has his responses to each.

The joy is, "Blessed are all who take refuge in him." That implies there will be opportunity for individual response. In contrast, a national government decides our response in giving taxes, but each of us decides his or her own personal response to our God.

What is man that you are mindful of him, the son of man that you care for him? You made him a little lower than the heavenly beings and crowned him with glory and honor. (Psalm 8:4–5)

For what little that we understand, God could have chosen not to make men and women. Yet he made both and chose to be very attentive to them. That is humbling when we try to conceive that the One Distinct God takes "time" and "effort" to be aware, to give guidance and to show love to us. Have we ever been surprised by someone we did not know well, who went out of his or her way to do a favor? Let us be amazed that God steps out of his way to favor us.

We are to rule over all that is around us on this earth. How gracious of God. We may not be doing well at this assignment, but we do have the responsibility.

We are high on his list. We are only below him and angels. Yes, we are higher than turtles that live 150 years and than trees that live two and three thousand years. Then earthly age is not a criterion for worth in God's sight. We, people, are indeed crowned with glory and honor by attentiveness and love.

Let not pride well up within us. Join with David in his opening and closing words of this Psalm, "O Lord, our Lord, how majestic is your name in all the earth!"

Surely goodness and love will follow me all the days of my life, and I will dwell in the house of the Lord forever. (Psalm 23:6)

God has an extensive plan for us.

Phase 1 is to care for us in this earthly life. We have many related expressions such as in Psalm 18 where God is described as our Rock, Fortress, Deliverer, Refuge, Shield, Horn of Salvation and Stronghold. God saves us from enemies, hears our cries for help, arms us with strength, makes our feet like the feet of deer, trains our hands and broadens our path. There is responsibility on our part since, at times, we grieve God and must turn back to him with repentance. God gives wave upon wave of his grace. In Psalm 29:11 we read: "The Lord gives strength to his people; the Lord blesses his people with peace."

Phase 2 is to lead us from this life into the everlasting life. That means being with him. Note the word "salvation," which occurs more than forty times in the Psalms. Its connotation reaches from present physical help to eternal benefit. David here refers to living in "the house of the Lord." That's far better than saying that we will live in Jim's or Betty's house, for neither will live forever. Can we tell God that, in trusting him, we know that we will be with him forever?

God is our Shepherd, starting now and reaching into eternity. Jump for joy! Read on for what's next.

Many, O Lord my God, are the wonders you have done. The things you planned for us...Then I said, "Here I am, I have come—it is written about me in the scroll. To do your will, O my God, is my desire." (Psalm 40:5, 7–8)

Yes, God, the wonders you have done for us are "too many to declare." Yes, you would rather have us completely do your will than offer animal sacrifices (had we been living at that time) for sins of disobedience. We admit, time and again, that we do not do your will completely.

Would we worship anyone we found who really does God's will? David must be writing about someone other than himself. "Written about me in the scroll" must be a reference to previous hints in the scrolls written by Moses and the judges as to someone special to come. Surely David is not boasting about himself with "Here I am!"

David spoke with such certainty, as though that person stood before him. Prophets often spoke that way, as though the future event were happening at that moment. David gave such hope for this special One. Was he referring to a son, grandson or an heir some generations later? We'll need to wait and see.

No man can redeem the life of another or give to God a ransom for him—the ransom for a life is costly, no payment is ever enough—that he should live on forever and not see decay....But God will redeem my soul from the grave; he will surely take me to himself. (Psalm 49:7–9, 15)

In the midst of our frequent boasting among folk, suddenly here is such a serious thought. No human can take the place of another to satisfy God; no one can muster the price of ransom. Surely there is some method of rising above the animal sacrifices for atonement—a method of arranging to live on forever. All cultures have suggestions to that end.

Since all peoples crave to live on forever, can't one turn to any god? We dare not. This message thus far indicates that the God who made the world, made humans with the ability to respond to him. The God who formed this Hebrew nation has made a certain promise over and over again. This God has promised that a special Person will come! God revealed his intent to Adam and Eve, and to several others throughout the centuries. Just a few pages back, in Psalm 40, David wrote prophetically of one, "Here I am, I have come...." One, not David, assumes this role: "God will redeem my soul,...will surely take me to himself." When would this Person come? We don't know (thus far in our sequence through the Bible). The serious question is: Will we recognize and accept the One when sent? We must read on.

When you ascended on high, you led captives...; you received gifts from men, even from the rebellious....Our God is a God who saves; from the Sovereign Lord comes escape from death. (Psalm 68:18–20)

Again David seems to be speaking of someone different than—greater than—a human. Is this One only to ride in some spectacular way from mountain top to mountain top accompanied by thousands of chariots? Neighboring nations supposed their gods dwelled in the trees or on the mountain tops. How are we sure David's God is different or better?

Go beyond the pomp. This one will "captivate" us, maybe quite literally. That, too, is not new among gods. This one will receive gifts, even from the rebellious. That's quite surprising that there will be recognition given even by rebellious people.

There is more. This God bears our burdens, even saves. Often "save" is used simply for "save my skin" from harm or death. This is the Sovereign Lord—the first occurrence of "sovereign" in the Psalms. How sovereign? In him is escape from death!

Escape from death! The Psalmist (Chp. 49) already indicated that a special Person would escape death. Now the Psalmist bears the good news that we have the chance to miss death. Hooray, we don't understand how it will happen, but we'll buy that! Next...

Show us your unfailing love, O Lord, and grant us your salvation....Surely his salvation is near those who fear him, that his glory may dwell in our land. (Psalm 85:7–9)

Many Psalms mention *salvation.* God is David's Salvation and elicits his praise (18:1–3). David will not have fear, does have confidence and will wait patiently (27:1, 13–14). Such joy in salvation bursts forth in testimony to people and in exaltation to God. (40:1, 16) David speaks so assuredly (62:1–2) that Salvation is from God only. That comes from the five-star general, David. He is not lauding his own leadership, wealth, wisdom or prestige. He simply says from the heart that salvation is of God, even implying that it is a gift. David also indicates it is available to people beyond Israel (67:1–2).

In Psalm 85, the lyricist speaks lovingly and directly to God: "You...You...You...." God's abundant love will naturally bear fruit in salvation, including the elusive quality of peace. The worshiping people are even called *saints.* This gives self-worth to lives. These people had a reverent awe for God.

As we praise God in exaltation and reverent awe, let us not put any bees in our bouquets by reminding God of our own claims. As sure as God's unfailing love, so is God's salvation. We will have peace and not anxiety. Amen.

For he will command his angels concerning you to guard you in all your ways. "Because he loves me," says the Lord, "I will rescue him; I will protect him, for he acknowledges my name." (Psalm 91:9–16; cf. Exodus 23:20–23)

God uses angels to help us in this life. We seek to eat properly and drive carefully for self-preservation. God knows that and, yes, he also arranges angels for certain aspects of protection. We can't measure that protection. Perhaps that is why we ignore this provision.

Moses records (Exodus 23:20–23) the Lord's announcement that an angel was given to guard Israel along their way, to direct them to the land and to overcome six nations. God's imprimatur was upon the angel. We have already read of other occasions of angels helping on particular missions.

The psalmist here, likely Moses, begins with the thought of protection from God. He charges angels to "guard you in all your ways." Astounding!

Isn't it humbling that there are some things that we cannot measure? That does not make the presence of angels any less real. No thought is expressed of addressing or worshiping the angels, just gratitude for their instrumentality. Let's expect God's use of them on our behalf today. Thank You, God. Next.

The Lord has sworn and will not change his mind: "You are a priest forever, in the order of Melchizedek." (Psalm 110:4. Reread Genesis 14:18)

Abraham went on a rescue mission and defeated the main enemy. The allied kings met with Abraham. Melchizedek, king of Salem (Salem became Jerusalem), brought bread and wine for the returning warriors. He was also the priest for God Most High. He declared blessing upon Abraham, who responded by giving one tenth of everything he had captured.

This was a fresh encounter in the midst of the multitude of neighboring national gods. Abraham trusted Melchizedek because he represented the God-Creator. Melchizedek means *King of Righteousness.* Abraham did not know his lineage.

Centuries later, the Psalmist uses this name as a type. A very special Person will come and have a place of honor with God (vs.1) and be a great king-warrior. Also, this One will be a priest of the type of Melchizedek. This assignment is as fixed as can be—by God's oath. He will not change his mind.

We so desperately need such a priest. Melchizedek was a shining one in the midst of what was corrupt. This One to come will have continued existence and will combine the office of king and priest, as did Melchizedek. This combination of king and priest was not allowed in David's time. God, please show us this One, for we do need a priest.

The stone the builders rejected has become the capstone; the Lord has done this....Blessed is he who comes in the name of the Lord. From the house of the Lord we bless you. (Psalm 118:22–26)

As one builds a stone wall, stones are selected by size and shape. Often, several stones are set aside in order to choose the right one for the next placement. Surely the author here does not mean stones literally, for he is talking about the relationship of righteousness. We have not found Abraham, Isaac, Jacob, Moses, judges or kings who could present a righteous relationship with Holy God. It seems that when we find the right One, we will be confident of personal salvation.

But the author says that the builders reject the One who is truly the capstone. Does that mean that the people who have the skill to recognize the One God chooses will reject that one? In spite of that, apparently when God shows this One, many people will consider it marvelous. Those people will rejoice and rejoice.

The car license plate indicates from whence a person has come. This One will be evident, in some way, as having come from the Lord. He can even use the name of the Lord! We give thanks, Lord, but please give us more specific information.

Where can I go from your Spirit? Where can I flee from your presence? (Psalm 139:7)

Whenever we try to flee from God, something is wrong. We become like the youngster, having been told not to take any cookies, who hides from Mother's presence upon taking the cookies.

Instead, suppose a difficult circumstance, not of our choosing, has led us to wonder if God's Spirit could possibly be with us. Consider David's conclusion, "Neither height nor depth nor land nor sea could remove him from God's Spirit." David had prayed (Psalm 51:11), "Do not...take your Holy Spirit from me," yet was certain he would not. In David's Psalms we begin to realize that, as David spoke on the one hand for himself, yet his expressions are representative of mankind. David says things we wish we could express for ourselves. We begin to realize that God's Spirit is present and helps people who are seeking God and trying to obey him.

Something strange seems to be unfolding before us: God's Spirit can function on our behalf without a body of his own. The Spirit comes upon our bodies. We cannot flee; neither do we want to.

David may have written when he was young, shepherding sheep, or when he was older, shepherding people as king for forty years. Whenever, we're so glad he wrote.

CONVERSATIONAL PRAYER

These five books—Job through Song of Solomon (Song of Songs)—are called the Poetical Books. There is much more personal emotion shared in these. Can we, too, let out some feelings by informal prayer? It may seem to ramble, and that's all right.

Thank you, God, that you caused these books to be in your Book. You showed that others ahead of me have had deep questions and a wide range of feelings. Thanks for Job and his examples of struggle, anger and patience all mixed together. I understand so little of your method of testing in this life. I'll try to be patient. Thanks, God, for such a man as David—having been an excellent warrior and leader, yet with a depth of feelings as shown in poetry and song. How well he represents me in saying things I wouldn't dare. That helps me vent my hurts. That helps me praise you as I walk, as I ride or drive, and as I wash dishes. You indicate that a special One will come who will rightly use your name. In the meantime, you gave another great human, Solomon. How beautifully he used his brilliance for your purpose. I wonder if he could have lived on Satan's side instead? Maybe such a fear prompted his writing so many precautions which are for me, too. Also, I'll try not to make pleasure, work, riches, prestige, wisdom or any other earthly circumstance my god; not even my spouse whom I adore with words and deeds. Please be patient with me. I don't understand all that you have planned for me.

(What excitement and confidence do you have from going through the Bible thus far? Tell God, using your own words of prayer.)

PROPHETICAL

Therefore the Lord himself will give you a sign: The virgin will be with child and will give birth to a son, and will call him Immanuel. (Isaiah 7:14)

We have come to the large segment of the Old Testament called the Prophets. Isaiah is thought to have lived and written in the eighth century before Christ. Prophets tell forth and often foretell. Isaiah had already told forth strong words of judgment and now foretells this sign from God.

A virgin is to be with child. What a way to draw snickers and laughter! How is a young woman to have her parents or closest friends believe that? Now wait, Isaiah said this was God's sign. Any notice is based upon the character of the person making said notice; in this case, God. This would indeed get our attention as being an act of God or else a sad joke.

This virgin would give birth to a son. That's a fifty-fifty chance of being correct. Again, wait, the first child shall be a son—100% certainty! If the message from the prophet is not correct, then he is not God's prophet.

The name for this Son will be Immanuel. That means, *God with us.* Then, this Person in a human body will also be God! That rules out the current wonderful King Hezekiah. Have we ever clung to a statement a friend made; hoping it was true, yet fearful it would not come about? Let's cling to God's statement.

For to us a child is born, to us a son is given, and the government will be on his shoulders. And he will be called Wonderful Counselor, Mighty God, Everlasting Father, Prince of Peace. (Isaiah 9:6)

Did we call Solomon "Wonderful Counselor" considering the writings he left us—Proverbs, Ecclesiastes and Song of Songs? No, even Job reminded us that God is our Counselor.

Is "Mighty God" an appellation for a human king? Blasphemy! God directed Isaiah to announce this, since man, in the midst of his utter shortfall, needs a very special God-Person.

How could "Everlasting Father" possibly apply to one in human form? Isaiah, your credibility as a prophet is on the line. Why didn't the Hebrew people imprison you for your writing? God in human form?

We've had "princes of peace" before, for forty or fifty years at a time. We are impressed that Isaiah says this One will extend peace for a long time, perhaps through the duration of this earth.

This is a promise that benefits Gentiles, too. Remember Abraham's special offspring? A problem, though, lies not with God—as to how he will bring all this to pass—but with us, in accepting this Person when he is made known. Will our self-made expectations hinder our acceptance?

What's next?

A shoot will come up from the stump of Jesse; from his roots a branch will bear fruit....In that day the Root of Jesse will stand as a banner for the peoples; the nations will rally to him. (Isaiah 11:1–10)

Sure, sprouts often grow out of a stump after a tree is cut. Since Jesse is a person, this must be an illustration of an offspring of Jesse. Someone, generations later, will be special and be called a *Branch*. Read on. "The Spirit of the Lord will be on him." Qualities superior to human will be his. He will make righteous judgments without relying upon outward appearances. There will be some time when he will slay the wicked by his spoken word.

More? Indeed. Animals of many sorts will be able to live together amicably! A child will lead a calf and a lion, together. I remember that picture on the wall of my childhood bedroom. And nations will come to this special One. There will be a general assembly of Hebrew people from all over the earth. Changes in the earth's geography will occur.

All that is very awesome. It must be for the good of people or else you would not do those things, God. Surely this includes our salvation. We'll try to take your hand in trust, God, as a child takes a parent's hand when frightened.

He will swallow up death forever. The Sovereign Lord will wipe away the tears from all faces; he will remove the disgrace of his people from all the earth. The Lord has spoken. (Isaiah 25:8)

We understand that a whale swallows fish. We somewhat understand that a black hole in space "swallows" matter. But, Isaiah says there will be an occasion when death will be swallowed up! The Lord will do this. Our human body will cease to face its foreboding death mode. On a certain mountain there will be a display in view of multitudes. The "how" is not elaborated, but the benefits are made clear. Look at 26:19: "...Dead will live." Isaiah was inspired by God to write all this about twenty-seven centuries ago.

Mother often wipes away her child's tears following physical or emotional hurts. "Mommy, I cut my finger....Mommy, my friend wouldn't walk home with me today." Our love wipes away some tears, but God's tender love will wipe away all tears. May some of our tears be from realizing the way we have treated others, and may our deepest tears be from knowing how we offended God. Reread the Psalmist's visualization in 130:3, "Who could stand?" If we can't, at times, fall into tearful sorrow for our offenses, perhaps we haven't come close to God!

God will wipe away all tears and disgrace, and at that moment we will be OK in our hearts and in his. When will this take place?

So this is what the Sovereign Lord says: "See, I lay a stone in Zion, a tested stone, a precious cornerstone for a sure foundation; the one who trusts will never be dismayed." (Isaiah 28:16)

When man lays a cornerstone, he shows promise of something to be built. People nearby look forward to the completion, for when the ABC Company occupies the building, there will be a benefit to the community in services performed and in increased employment. There is trust for what will be in the future.

The Stone that God offers us is even better. It is tested, precious and sure. It is tested for strength of character, precious in God's eyes and hopefully in man's, and sure as a base for God's plan of accomplishments. Will a manufactured product suffice as this cornerstone—a human service, a philosophy, a policing or military force? None of the above. For this is God's arrangement. This cornerstone must be a Person, for the results are personal. Anyone who trusts will not be dismayed, for death will be annulled!

We have thought of Son-Immanuel as a Person; Counselor-God-Father-Prince as a Person; One with wisdom, understanding, counsel, power and knowledge as a Person; and the One who overrides death as a Person. This Cornerstone must be all of the above.

When, Lord?

And a highway will be there; it will be called the Way of Holiness....But only the redeemed will walk there,...Everlasting joy will crown their heads. Gladness and joy will overtake them, and sorrow and sighing will flee away. (Isaiah 35:8–10)

In this chapter, Isaiah is at first speaking of physical, earthly things and then extends his thoughts to things of the future—even eternal future. There will be a special way of life. There will be discrimination! Now don't back away—God selects, we don't. Only the redeemed will walk there; that's why I want to listen to God's plan, for "I want to be in that number, when the saints go marchin' in!" Note that the selection is not by nation or race.

Oh, I want to be there. There will be no "ferocious beast" which might imply that there will not be the accidents that happen in this life. And Satan will not be there? I will have everlasting joy and gladness. Sorrow and regrets will be gone. "God, I have caused other people sorrow and regrets, and I have brought more than a little sorrow upon myself. Thank you, that somehow you will bring about a clean sweep."

We have watched a cook use a colander to drip out the undesired water and grit, but retain the main food. With sorrow gone, gladness and joy will remain so prominent. Tell us more, Isaiah.

Comfort, comfort my people, says your God....They will soar on wings like eagles; they will run and not grow weary, they will walk and not be faint. (Isaiah 40:1, 31)

Isaiah, you make such grandiose statements involving people and the universe. People will change their weapons into agricultural tools? (2:4). But, we see people always at war. There will be user-friendly smoke and fire from Mt. Zion? (4:5–6). An erupting mountain hardly seems friendly. And, of all things, the stars won't be seen? (13:10). How many in the neighborhood laughed when you said these things? The moon and the sun, they, too, will be changed? (24:23). That would mean drastic ecological changes. No one will be ill? (33:24). Man isn't doing nearly that well with medicines. Isaiah, you are certainly outdoing the prophets of Baal. Please don't tease us.

No, we can't manipulate the bulk of this earth (Chp. 40). We certainly can't comprehend the Spirit, let alone instruct him. True, none of us are on God's advisory committee to receive his ideas for our approval. "Yes, yes, God, from the beginning we have realized you are above all possibility of the earth affecting you. We sort of understand you; but the things you say you will do—those are the things that confuse us. We join the Psalmist, 'Be still, and know that I am God' (46:10). Then, we will be comforted and will 'soar on wings like eagles...walk and not be faint.'"

Here is my servant, whom I uphold, my chosen one in whom I delight; I will put my Spirit on him and he will bring justice to the nations....And new things I declare; before they spring into being I announce them to you. (Isaiah 42:1, 9)

How strange that this Servant to come will have contrasting personality characteristics. Look back also at 40:10–11, one will rule yet be tender as a shepherd. In the present passage, he will be a servant yet bring justice to nations. This is more than a man. Man can be strong in the manner of ruling and be roughshod over feelings. Man can be tender and not be chosen to be a ruler. Surely only the One from God by his Spirit will have all these qualities.

Who is behind this? God who made the heavens and earth and has managed the peoples of this earth. All of his power is available to bring all this to pass. God will place this servant here in righteousness and make him to be a covenant for people, even for Gentiles. There already was a covenant with the Hebrew people, hence this must mean there will be a new covenant to include Gentiles. Good news!

God does not share his name or glory with another, yet he announces this Servant-Person as being so much like himself. But these things did not come to pass in Isaiah's time. God, surely you're not finished explaining.

Before me no god was formed, nor will there be one after me. I, even I, am the Lord, and apart from me there is no savior. I have revealed and saved and proclaimed—I, and not some foreign god among you. You are my witnesses. (Isaiah 43:10–12)

A contest is before us. On the one hand, people of other nations try to put forth their record of things foretold. On the other hand, the Lord declares that the Hebrew nation itself is his witness and is a servant with a record over many centuries of God's announcements coming to pass. The result is that many people believe in this God. There is no contest, really.

No real god preceded God, nor will any follow him. No other made heaven and earth, nor guided a nation foretelling judgments and rewards, nor used a covenant over the centuries, nor promised a Savior. There is no comparison.

God foretold, even centuries in advance, of matters actually coming to pass. From those things that have come about, we have confidence for those matters that are now only partially accomplished. Time and again God saved the king and nation from their wayward course. He has promised a Savior for eternity and has given a few characteristics pertaining to a new earth and eternity. We must wait for further explanation in his time. God, we'll join with the witnesses that you are the One.

This is what the Lord says to his anointed, to Cyrus, "…I will go before you…so that you may know that I am the Lord, the God of Israel, who calls you by name.…I am the Lord, and there is no other; apart from me there is no god." (Isaiah 45:1–7)

God had a unique reason to speak to Cyrus, king of Persia, a Gentile king. God chose Cyrus to be an agent and led him to victories so that he would know that God is God. Historians tell us that Cyrus did have success. God chose him also to benefit Israel. Cyrus did indeed benefit the Hebrews, "The Lord, the God of heaven,…has appointed me to build a temple for him at Jerusalem" (Ezra 1:2. Re-read all of Ezra).

Note the astounding titles God gave him: My shepherd (44:28) and anointed. In the Hebrew, anointed is Messiah! In the Greek version (Septuagint), it is Christ! But God, surely Cyrus is not the Anointed One you promised. This Cyrus has only a human role; so we'll still wait for the One.

Can we allow that God may have a vital role for a government that seems to us to be very heathen? For example, a variety of religions were represented by the nations that established the nation Israel in 1948. A benefit for Israel today? Yes.

It is too small a thing for you to be my servant....I will also make you a light for the Gentiles, that you may bring my salvation to the ends of the earth (Isaiah 49:6). *See, I will beckon to the Gentiles, I will lift up my banner to the peoples* (49:22).

The "servant" is sometimes Israel as a whole and sometimes a reference to the specific God-Person promised to us. Let us move from the Servant to the mission. The breadth of his mission is indicated in the opening of this paragraph at verse 1, as he beckons people of islands and distant nations to hearken to his announcement. It is too small an assignment for this Servant to be the means of benefiting only the tribes of Israel. The mission is far more expansive, benefiting also the Gentiles. I am so glad because this includes me. Remember that this extensive mission was declared as early as Abraham (Genesis 12:3).

Isn't it encouraging when a friend beckons with the hand for us to come, as opposed to one who, with the back of the hand (in some cultures the left hand is used), motions for us to depart? In our rural society, we hang a banner across Main Street to invite people to a rodeo. God beckons with his hand and also lifts a banner across our road of life to invite us to his salvation!

Lift up your eyes to the heavens, look at the earth beneath; the heavens will vanish like smoke....But my salvation will last forever, my righteousness will never fail....But my righteousness will last forever, my salvation through all generations. (Isaiah 51:6–8)

Isaiah had just said there would be great benefits for the Hebrew people, and then says that the earth will lose its purpose and the peoples will die in large numbers. He does not tell us how or when.

Through all of that, two things will last: salvation and righteousness. They will last through the remaining generations of man and into forever. Isaiah refers to salvation almost as frequently as the psalmists. "Let us rejoice and be glad in his salvation" (Isaiah 25:9). "God makes salvation" (Isaiah 26:1). The criterion seems to be to have "my law in your hearts" (Isaiah 51:7).

How glad we are that God did not ask for a certain percentage of obedience to his law. Because by any such standard, we would fail and not be accepted. On the one hand, we do keep God's love and law as principles in our hearts daily. Though, on the other hand, we frequently disobey in deeds. We don't want to cling to some weak thing that surely will become dilapidated later, so we cling to God's righteousness and salvation that won't weaken or change. They will last and last!

Who has believed our message?...For he bore the sin of many, and made intercession for the transgressors. (Isaiah 53)

Is this the special One we are to believe? He would come from an unlikely place, seem to be quite commonplace, and have no apparent characteristic or station to recommend him (vs.2). He would come to be despised by many and would experience extreme suffering (vs.3). Somehow, he would take upon himself our sins (and, we hope, all guilt) and in some way would even seem to be rejected by God (vs.4). He would be killed for our sins, and his substitute punishment would bring us peace with God (vs.5). Yes, I understand that each one of us has sinned, but how would the guilt of all of us be placed against only One?

He would be led to his death as though he could not prevent it; yet, there would be something voluntary about it (vs.7). He would be taken from man's manipulation to accomplish God's purpose—to cover the guilt of his people (vs.8). He would completely die as evidenced by entombment (vs.9). All would work toward God's intention for good, and somehow this one will continue to live and see in us the results of his death (vs.10). He, the Righteous Servant, would justify many people by bearing their iniquity (vs.11). Hooray, thereby is our salvation and righteous position! Isaiah said it again: This special one would die to carry away my sin, that is, die in my place.

God, we want to meet our Savior!

The Spirit of the sovereign Lord is on me, because the Lord has anointed me....For he has clothed me with garments of salvation and arrayed me in a robe of righteousness....So the Sovereign Lord will make righteousness and praise spring up before all nations. (Isaiah 61)

This One declares that the Spirit is on him and now he can truly be called the Anointed One. He is clothed with salvation and righteousness. He loves justice and will not stand aloof, but will reward people. What will he bestow?

The long list of changes he will bring to lives is good news. There will be freedom, release, comfort, beauty, gladness and praise. We will be called priests, each believer having direct access to God! The Anointed One will make an everlasting covenant a new covenant reaching out to all nations. No human leader can do these things—bridge nations and races, and bring benefit equally to all. Thank you, God, for doing what man cannot.

The Anointed One, being clothed with salvation and righteousness, indicates he will bestow salvation and righteousness upon the believers. We sometimes nickname our government Uncle Sam, as the one who bestows material benefits upon us. God has made this Anointed One to give God's great spiritual benefits of salvation and righteousness.

Behold, I will create new heavens and a new earth. The former things will not be remembered, nor will they come to mind. But be glad and rejoice forever in what I will create. (Isaiah 65:17–25)

As we read through this, can we exclaim, "Isaiah, surely God gave us this vision!" Thank God he announced that out of Abraham's offspring would come a benefit to the Gentiles, and that when the Servant would come there would be benefit to the nations. This must be a New Jerusalem for all believers.

No occasion will arise to cause weeping or crying. Even former things that so often brought regrets will not be remembered. Amazing! Length of life will be vastly longer. There will not be infant death. The age of one hundred will be youthful. Work will bring its proper reward for a person enjoying his own harvest and home. This will go on and on. Neither child nor adult will face threats of doom by man's holocausts. God will have an intimacy of communication with us and will delight in us. Somehow God will change animals so that they will not use each other as prey. Perhaps the rest of nature will change.

God, we are ready to be "glad and rejoice forever in what [you] will create!"

At that time they will call Jerusalem The Throne of the Lord, and all nations will gather in Jerusalem to honor the name of the Lord. No longer will they follow the stubbornness of their evil hearts. (Jeremiah 3:17)

A unity of nations will occur in Jerusalem. This is humbling, for in spite of all the effort in this century, from the League of Nations to the United Nations to common markets, no real unity has taken place. These are man's best efforts. However, in the future, all nations will gladly meet in Jerusalem, not New York or Hong Kong. They will not be acting out of greed. This will be God's best work. Astounding! Will we live to see this?

The surprising part of this revelation is that Jerusalem will be the center for God's presence. The old ark of the covenant will not be there, and the Hebrew people won't miss it. There will be some kind of throne dedicated to the Lord, or the entire city will be as the throne. There will not be a syncretism of the world's religions. Only the Lord will be lifted up. Even the Hebrew people will have a sense of unity. Why should all this take place at Jerusalem? Because the Lord chose the Hebrew people. Why did he choose them? Out of his great love. Why will God let you and me into his salvation and righteousness? Out of His great love.

This is what the Lord says, "...Call to me and I will answer you and tell you great and unsearchable things you do not know." (Jeremiah 33:2–3)

As though a pearl fell out of a bag, here is an amazing gem—a request by God. He tells the people to talk to him. Don't wait until you're in a problem and want out, as in the old fox-hole religion. No busy signal, no number disconnected, no recording machine service. Some people think things are too big to mention to God; whereas others think they must solve half the problem in their own strength before asking God; and some utilize a poor sense of humility, assuming some things are too small. CALL!

I WILL ANSWER YOU. Answering has at least three choices: yes, no and wait. We've already seen that, often, God announces a plan and then waits centuries to bring it to fruition. In personal lives, God, at times, indicates "wait, to regain your strength or health." Often we think we have not heard a "Yes" or "No" from God. Hasn't a friend or spouse said to you, "You're not listening"? May we admit that there needs to be personal growth in listening for God's answers.

The telling of great and unsearchable things you can't possibly know of your own self—time and again God presented his mind to humans—that is revelation.

Next!

In those days and at that time I will make a righteous Branch sprout from David's line.... This is the name by which it will be called: The Lord our Righteousness. (Jeremiah 33:15–16. Review Isaiah 4:2; 11:1–2, 10)

Isaiah indicates that a Branch, a special Person, will come who will be beautiful and glorious and will benefit the people with crops consistent and generous. This Branch will arise out of the kingdom that failed, as a tree becomes diseased and falls. Why herald this One? Only in him there is hope. This person will have the Spirit as evident in wisdom and understanding, in counsel and power, and in knowledge and fear of the Lord. How this person can be so God-like and yet in human form, we don't understand. How special and majestic. Obviously, this would be only by God's sovereign arrangement.

Jeremiah stresses that God will send the Branch. He will be of David's lineage, will bring justice, will cause Israel to live in safety, and will have the alias, "The Lord Our Righteousness."

In all, this One is presented as desirable in God's mind, although he will be deprecated in the minds of many people. This warns us—even today—that we are not to say, "I'll decide for myself whether or not I like your arrangement." Do we really want this One without adding our own conditions? Be prepared to revel in this One who is for us and for all nations.

Because of the Lord's great love we are not consumed, for his compassions never fail. They are new every morning....I will wait for him. (Lamentations 3:22–24)

Anytime we become smug before God, just read verse 22 and Psalm 130:3 again. How it is that a person can walk over hot coals and not be burned? We don't know. How is it that one can commune with God and not be destroyed? We only know it is because of his love, his compassionate love. For joining a club, one needs references indicating how good the person is. When joining a Christian church, one presents the opposite: his own confession, "I am not good before God; I am a sinner." His compassion is new every dawn.

So, you lost the ball game yesterday. Today, your team will play again with the score starting at 0-to-0. During your day, count the "hits" that God makes for you—protection, guidance, mental and moral strength. Did you start the day with a big portion of a certain cereal? For spiritual strength, God is to be your "big" portion.

Some people misconstrue "wait" as idleness. However, we still have the human responsibility of planning and trying. In the midst of doing our part, we are to have patience with God's arrangements. I know a woman who was serving the Lord in a lovely way when a particular incident caused serious back trouble. She thoughtfully listened to the suggestions for surgery and then did so. She did what could be done humanly, and, also, cheerfully awaits what additional changes God will bring about, knowing the final outcome is by God.

> *Then they will know that I am the Lord their God, for though I sent them into exile among the nations, I will gather them to their own land, not leaving any behind....I will pour out my Spirit on the house of Israel....* (Ezekiel 39:28–29. Reread 11:10–19; 16:59; 20:34; 28:25; 34:11; 36:24; 37:21)

Several times Ezekiel has presented the concept of the Hebrew people being returned to their land from the Babylonian captivity (6th century B.C.). Is that mundane as a past event completed, or are there ramifications for Hebrew people of today and tomorrow?

Ezekiel 11:17 refers simply to the return from the Babylonian captivity. Later, Ezekiel 28:25–26 says God would gather the people and show his presence before the nations. Israel would live in safety while God punished neighboring nations. Again, Ezekiel 34:11–16 portrays God as a Shepherd ruling with justice. Ezekiel 36:24–28 adds to the gathering a cleansing and instilling of a new Spirit in their hearts for obedience. He mentions (37:21–28) the unity of the restored nation, the closeness of God, that one like David will rule and that there will be a new everlasting covenant. At last (39:28–29), God will gather his people and give his Spirit. Since these matters don't seem to exist, Ezekiel must be referring to events surrounding a return of the Hebrews at some time later than from Babylon, and yet ahead of us.

Let's glance back at Isaiah 11:10–16. He refers to a second return from several countries and from the whole earth. God will even alter nature. People of other nations will have some kind of benefit. Even Jeremiah 23:3–8 mentions a remnant, a Branch-King-Lord of Righteousness, a gathering of throngs from the world (31:8), and Israel's guilt being removed (50:19–20). Both of these authors mention more than what happened upon returning from Babylon.

Hence, God was foretelling another return from neighboring countries. There will be righteous leadership by a God-Person. Guilt will be gone. A special Spirit will be evident, resulting in obedience. Some nations will be affected adversely, whereas other peoples will receive an unexplained benefit.

What has happened in recent history? Israel was declared by many countries to be a nation on May 14, 1948. Throngs of Hebrew people from many countries have since returned to the land, and some Gentiles as well. Hallelujah! However, other promised events, such as safety and the Just Ruler, have not yet come to pass. We observe that God's promises may take place in various stages.

How will we recognize God's Spirit and the particular covenant? God, you have the habit of letting us wait until fruition for your revelation. We'll try to anticipate, and yet be patient.

All the peoples of the earth are regarded as nothing. He does as he pleases with the powers of heaven and the peoples of the earth. No one can hold back his hand. (Daniel 4:35)

Who exclaimed this? Nebuchadnezzar, a Gentile! Earlier he had been a very proud ruler, "I have built....My mighty power....My majesty...." God's voice countered with the declaration that he would become like an animal for seven years. The purpose seemed to be to show rulers that God is sovereign over kingdoms.

Immediately (a day? a week?) he was driven out of his position and away from the people. He lived in the habitat of an animal. Astounding! Once in a while, such a person has been found and brought back into civilization. However, the return of habits and stature comes slowly. Hence, even more astounding that, after seven years, Nebuchadnezzar was quite immediately returned to normal mental and physical abilities.

He rose up and declared that God is in control of people, that God has an eternal dominion over this earth, that God decides what he wants to do, and that God is not held back by man. He may not intervene in such a spectacular way as with Nebuchadnezzar, but he can if he wishes.

Try verse 37 for today's motto: "I, (put in your name), praise and exalt and glorify the King of heaven."

There before me was one like a son of man, coming with the clouds of heaven. He approached the Ancient of Days and was led into His presence. He was given authority, glory and sovereign power; all peoples, nations and men of every language worshiped him. His dominion is an everlasting dominion. (Daniel 7:13–14)

Daniel, after describing four beasts of enormous power on earth, sees the Ancient of Days—evidently, God. Then he sees One like a son of man, very distinct from the beasts and yet distinct from common man, for this One was accepted into God's presence. This Son of Man will be given authority, glory and God-power to show to people of all language groups, who then will worship him. Daniel wrote what God revealed.

We have already had the "Son of Man" expression used by Ezekiel almost one hundred times. Ezekiel was a definitive spokesman for God. Yet, there is no worship of Ezekiel, for he remains humanly a son of man. Daniel's writing overlaps Ezekiel's (6th century B.C.). Both use "Son of Man" to describe the Supreme Person. Daniel emphasizes that there will be a new and everlasting kingdom. This Son of Man will be the king. The saints of God who enter the kingdom will receive opposition for three and a half years. God will win and the saints will be secure. Will we recognize the Son of Man? We want to enter his kingdom.

At that time your people—everyone whose name is found written in the book—will be delivered. Multitudes who sleep in the dust of the earth will awake: some to everlasting life, others to shame and everlasting contempt. (Daniel 12:1–2)

Michael—meaning *Who is like God?*—is an extraordinary angel and works to protect God's people through great distress. The previous chapters indicate warfare such as has not yet been experienced in our history. At God's chosen moment, Michael will deliver many people out of that distress. Also, multitudes of the dead will arise from "sleep" to being "awake."

An enormous distinction as to destiny is made by God's book. One group of people will receive everlasting life, while the other group receives everlasting contempt. The one condition is desirable, and the other is absolutely undesirable. (Compare Isaiah 66:24.)

The "book" is not a new subject. Moses referred to God's book containing the names of those whose sins are forgiven (Exodus 32:32). David referred to God's book of life as listing the righteous (Psalm 69:28).

The Psalmist many times declares death to be a sleep. Sleep indicates a condition from which to awaken and the person will then have sameness as before. Daniel speaks of awakening to a differentness, not of reincarnation but of resurrection. Resurrection will be an entering into an everlasting desirable position. Hallelujah! It didn't happen in Daniel's time. When, Michael?

I will ransom them from the power of the grave; I will redeem them from death. Where, O death, are your plagues? Where, O grave, is your destruction? (Hosea 13:14)

God reminded the tribe of Ephraim that they "shall acknowledge no God but me, no Savior except me" (vs.4). Yet they changed and "became guilty of Baal worship" and "forgot me." God reminded of his care, then pronounced his wrath in lengthy fashion. In the midst of all this hard judgment, is a promise: "I will redeem them from death" (vs.14). The contrast is as though you were walking the ocean beach seeing the multitude of inanimate rocks when, suddenly, you see living creatures.

God will ransom. A ransom is a price paid, usually in a situation that should not have even taken place. It is a price willingly paid when ownership exists but the object is in the hands of the wrong party. God will ransom from the power of the grave—redeem from death! To redeem requires a redeemer. A redeemer can only be one who loves so much that he wishes to intervene. This reminds us of Boaz who, as kinsman-redeemer, paid a price for Ruth (Chp. 4). Redemption accomplishes a great contrast: a change from spiritual death to spiritual life.

To the two questions in the text, the answers are: O Death, God will be your plague; and, O Grave, God will be your destroyer. Nature says I'll die, but I say I'd like to live. God says each one of us has the opportunity to live forever. What must each of us do?

...Before the coming of the great and dreadful day of the Lord. And everyone who calls on the name of the Lord will be saved; for on Mount Zion and in Jerusalem there will be deliverance. (Joel 2:28–32)

We look forward to the day when we leave on a special vacation. God would like us to look forward to a special day of his making when he will set his Spirit upon all kinds of people, giving prophecies, dreams and visions which will bring joy in daily living. God will demonstrate his power in the heavens and on earth with radical contradictions to the usual operations of nature. It would seem to be for the lifting of God above any other god in a most indisputable way.

These wonders apparently will immediately precede and, hence, be a warning of, God's great and dreadful day; great for believers who look forward to it, but dreadful for nonbelievers.

Anyone who invokes the name of God (no need to join the nation Israel) will be saved. The means, already indicated to be a Person, will be located in Jerusalem. *Saved* implies benefit beyond earthly life, and deliverance from the judgment and the wrath of God. Let us, Jew and Gentile, call on the Lord. Ah, that's what each of us must do: trust, believe, in what God reveals.

We look forward to His coming! Next!

But you, Bethlehem Ephrathah, though you are small among the clans of Judah, out of you will come for me one who will be ruler over Israel. (Micah 5:2)

Bethlehem was just a small town overlooked by regal Jerusalem from its higher elevation. Likely, many laughed when Micah said that someone important would come out of Bethlehem.

Micah said One will come who will rule over Israel. Did that mean a five- or twenty-year rule, as other kings? This reminds us of Gideon who, when the angel approached him, humbly countered, "How can I save Israel? My clan is the weakest in Manasseh, and I am the least in my family." In spite of his insignificant background, he did splendidly in battle and in rule—for the land had peace for forty years (Judges 6). But Micah said that God had in mind an even better leader, from Bethlehem. Oh yes, that's where David was born, and the prophets many times said that a special person of the lineage of David would rule forever. Is that the one to whom Micah refers?

What does "origins are from of old, from ancient times" mean? This seems to be a promise of someone very different, conjuring up Melchizedek (Genesis 14; Psalm 110). No genealogy was given for him, yet Abraham honored him. How do all these pieces of the puzzle fit together? We must read on.

See, your king comes to you, righteous and having salvation, gentle and riding on a donkey, on a colt, the foal of a donkey. (Zechariah 9:9)

A King! How wonderful it would be to have a righteous king. Then the people would rally around and, with great strength, beat off the overpowering nations. The prophets had said many times that someone of the lineage of David would rule forever. How comforting that would be for the living generation and for the ones to follow. Micah had said the ruler would be of Bethlehem. He would also readily be associated with Jerusalem for that is the capital—the place for a king.

He is to ride into town on a young donkey, a beast of burden? That's certainly not ostentatious; in fact, rather demeaning. If he is a conquering king, why not on a war horse? How can he bring peace to nations across the earth? Will there be lengthy negotiations? How many years and battles will that take?

All this seems impossible unless, Zechariah, God was revealing to you as he revealed to other prophets before you of the special person whom God would send. Then all of the above is readily possible, even salvation.

But, God, for centuries you have told the prophets to assure the people this special person would come. When? When? We've listened for so long already.

On that day there will be no light, no cold or frost. It will be a unique day....On that day living water will flow out from Jerusalem....On that day there will be one Lord, and his name the only name. (Zechariah 14:6–9)

Micah 4:1–5 declares that the mountain of the Lord's temple (referring to Mt. Zion in Jerusalem) will be prominent because people will flock to it to hear someone teaching God's ways. Quite obviously, it will not be a human teacher; for he will settle disputes between strong nations and they will not maintain war equipment. There will be security for the individual and a temporary tolerance for the gods of the nations.

Malachi 4:1–3 says there will be disaster for those who ignore God, whereas those who revere him will have strength and exuberance. He mentions God's great and dreadful day.

Zechariah describes that "Day": temperature and light will be changed, and a new water source will spring forth in Jerusalem. Unusual indeed, but most unique will be a visible presence of the Lord as ruler over the whole earth! Only His name will be used, and tolerance for other gods will be gone.

God, perhaps we are creating a blur by trying to merge what are separate future events. We fully trust you to bring about these wonders. We desire to be steadfast in worship of you while awaiting more explanations and the Day itself.

Then suddenly the Lord you are seeking will come to His temple; the messenger of the covenant, whom you desire, will come. (Malachi 3:1)

Let's try to combine several revelations about the Person. Micah says (5:2) that the little city of Bethlehem will present One who will rule over Israel. Zechariah has several observations saying (3:8–9; 6:12) that God will send his Servant, the Branch, and by him sin will be removed in a single day; and that (9:9) a King will come providing salvation. This great Person will ride on a lowly donkey. Then 11:12–13 adds another oddity, someone is paid thirty pieces of silver as the price for a person; but then he throws away the money. Is this a reference to the special Person? Mention is made (12:10) that One will be observed by the people, pierced and then mourned. The grief will be as for a first son.

Finally, Malachi announces a moment when God's representative, whom the people have been seeking, will come to the Temple and explain his covenant. God, you are undoubtedly telling us of only one special Person to come, not of a committee! We tend to ponder how all these pieces fit into one beautiful solution. But we long for Him with awe and do claim our salvation in Him.

CONVERSATIONAL PRAYER

We have skimmed through the books of Isaiah to Malachi. Isaiah to Daniel are called the Major Prophets. Hosea to Malachi are called the Minor Prophets. May we express the desire to grasp this special Person to come and through whom there will be everlasting salvation.

God, I am amazed! You used prophets to tell and retell the people to live differently. I tend to think I can get away with something because there is no prophet standing on the street corner today. Thank you for your patience, but I will try to be more obedient. I am amazed that you gave the script to the prophets, revealing what would be on stage in the next scenes. I realize that other gods are not able to do that. You have already, this century, brought back your remnant of people to form a visible nation. Perhaps there remains only a few, small acts of man until you will present the final scenes. My hair stands on end! You lifted a portion of the curtain and gave us glimpses of the Person. There are so many facets to Him that it is a wonder that one Actor can handle all the roles. Some of the conditions surrounding Him seem to be a "mission impossible." Your name is on the line. Yet, you have already brought so much to pass that I should not doubt the matters that are yet ahead. I don't understand how He can be you, and yet in human body form. That's the most amazing part. I think I am ready to meet Him. I want eternal life robed in your righteousness. In your name, I come just as I am.

(May you, in your own words, exuberantly express your confidence in this Person and in salvation and eternal life as you have learned from the prophets.)

BETWEEN
TESTAMENTS

PREPARATION FOR THE NEW TESTAMENT
Comments on the 400 years between the writing of Malachi and of Matthew.

The last of the prophets wrote, we believe, in the fifth century before Christ. The next four centuries are called the Silent Period, because none of the Bible books were written during those centuries. What happened in that era?

Intercontinental rule moved from Asia to Europe, from east to west. Persia ruled a vast area, including Israel. Then, Alexander the Great marched forth for Greece. Later, there were regional divisions. Even Egyptian and Syrian rulers had a hand on Jerusalem. Within Israel, a Maccabaean family led a series of revolts. Finally, in this series of grand empires, the Roman Empire ruled the scene. Rule had moved westward.

The Jews were often encouraged to move to cities of other nations, even to study in the great city of Alexandria. At times, they were encouraged to move back to Jerusalem. Many people respected the Jews for their high standard of behavior, industriousness and loyalty to a faith, and even joined with them as proselytes; others were fearful, jealous and worked hard to bring opposition.

Cultural change was significant. The Greek language became international. Highways were built and travel enhanced. The Scriptures—our Old Testament of 39 books—were translated (2nd and 3rd century B.C.) from Hebrew and Aramaic into Greek. This translation is nicknamed the Septuagint, for it is thought that there were about seventy people on the first translation committee; hence, the abbreviation: LXX.

There was much conflict between groups of Jews as to the interpretation of the Scriptures, and conflict regarding their response to changing political situations. As some Jews joined the Maccabaeans in revolt, others—the Essenes—claimed to keep the purity of the faith and withdrew socially. The Pharisees and Sadducees came into existence and became rivals. Pharisees, "The Separated Ones," were quite legalistic in applying the Scriptures to life and presented a little "holier than thou" attitude. They looked for the Messiah and believed in a resurrection. Sadducees, "The Righteous Ones," were the aristocratic cluster within the priesthood. They would collaborate with the Roman government, hold to the written Scriptures without the pharisaic legalism and deny a future resurrection.

The Jews were frequently fearful as to what lay ahead for them. Herod greatly improved the Temple and gave freedom to worship in the synagogues. Yet, there was much distrust, for Herod even asked that sacrifice be offered to him. He appointed "chief priests" not of Jewish choice. As he became old and ill, there was alarm as to a successor, for he had married many wives and had many sons.

In spite of these changes, the Jews steadfastly believed in one God, believed that God had chosen them to receive the special message of the Scriptures, meticulously copied the Scriptures, and thought that they were at some time to have a mission to the world. They looked forward to the coming of a special Person, Messiah, with mixed intent. Some supposed this One would be a king and would overthrow foreign political rule; others looked for him to change personal lives, even unto a resurrection.

We now turn to the New Covenant, or New Testament. Something will be changed or replaced so that our relationship with God will be quite new. Matters which were partially explained will be completely or much more so made clear. We will meet the same God, along with His Anointed One. Perhaps the greatest surprise will be the Holy Spirit. We will be reassured that the message is also for the Gentiles.

One thing more, you may want to make changes in your life. All of this we are to anticipate as we read God's New Covenant.

What will happen and when? What's next, Lord?

THREE
BIOGRAPHIES

All this took place to fulfill what the Lord had said through the prophet: "The virgin will be with child and will give birth to a son, and they will call him Immanuel"— which means, "God with us." (Matthew 1:22–23. Chapters 1–2)

Act II, Scene I: The Reconciler. Four accounts

Matthew directs our attention to someone important, not because of whom he knows, but because of his genealogy that stems from Abraham. Then Matthew tells us that Joseph accepted the angel's message that Mary would conceive by the Holy Spirit and, without doubt, have a son; and, of necessity because of his most unusual nature, call that son Jesus, Savior and Immanuel—God with us! Then this must be the One Isaiah told about centuries before (Isaiah 7:14). We await further evidence that he is more than man, is indeed God.

God next used an unnatural phenomenon in the sky to direct religious-philosophical travelers. They asked a ruler about a king within an ethnic group of his subjects. That seems bold. However, if they were right, then Micah of the Old Testament had the answer (5:2): find this special one in Bethlehem.

Four centuries had gone and no prophets had given further promises of the Special One. Now Matthew comes forthrightly bidding for our attention to this Jesus. The wealth of the gifts provided the means for the family to escape Herod's jealous intent to kill. Later, an angel told the family to move back. God was indeed making all the arrangements. Here is the One the prophets foretold! My God, you have my attention!

And a voice from heaven said, "This is my Son, whom I love; with him I am well pleased." (Matthew 3:17. Chapters 3–4)

Matthew next introduces John the Baptist. Isaiah, too, gave a hint of John centuries before (40:3). John was a strange man, not one to be chosen as a CEO of a big business; not likely one to have finished college—more the entrepreneur type. Instead of earning money, he gathers people about him with a jarring message: "Repent, for the kingdom of heaven is near." In what way is a kingdom near? There was no desirable, socially-correct government among the neighboring ethnic groups. Evidently this kingdom was near in time.

John speaks of one more powerful than himself. Whereas John applies water, the other one will apply the Holy Spirit. The Spirit of God was mentioned at times in the centuries past. Will the Holy Spirit be applied in some new way? Can a man do that? Yet this powerful one submits to the outward propriety of John's baptism. Immediately, God intervenes by voice to indicate his love and satisfaction. This Jesus is apparently superior to Abraham and Moses!

Amazing—a confrontation with the devil. Jesus rejected each offer of the devil on the basis of the Old Testament. Jesus indicated the Old Testament was the rule of his life and claimed to be superior to the devil!

Jesus repeats the message: "Repent, for the kingdom of heaven is near." Since Jesus is superior, if anyone will bring a new kingdom, surely he will.

But I tell you... (Matthew 5:22, 28, 32, 34, 39, 44. Chapters 5–7)

Jesus healed and spoke. News spread. He healed ones whom the doctors could not, and his ability certainly drew crowds. Yet he quickly indicated his primary purpose was teaching, and did so at length one particular day, giving what we call the Sermon on the Mount (Chapters 5–7).

If his teachings of lifestyles are serious, we're in deep trouble; we're not in that style—we're out. Jesus even struck down the mediocre living as taught by the religious leaders. Is this the kingdom of heaven—a radically different lifestyle? But we can't completely live up to that. We'll always be left out.

Even before we're certain we want to obey, Jesus bids us pray to God using "Father." That closeness appeals to us. But we need to forgive others? We don't like that. "Love your neighbor." We can try. "Love your enemy." We'll wait to see if the one who speaks it, does it. "Seek the kingdom." Obviously, there is a need for attentiveness, even intensity, on our part. Jesus stressed that: "Ask...seek...knock."

Why didn't many get up and walk away scoffing? There must have been something special about his person along with the directness and appealing wholesomeness of his words. The people were accepting him above their religious leaders! If only we could have been there; but instead, we'll have to listen to Matthew.

Are you the one who was to come, or should we expect someone else? ...Blessed is the man who does not fall away on account of me. (Matthew 11:3, 6. Chapters 8–11)

What a symphony of miracles and responses: healings of leprosy, paralysis, fever, blindness, deafness, calming storms, casting aside demons, raising from death to life. Truly, Isaiah's "man" is here "taking our infirmities" as none other! (Isaiah 53:4).

A Roman centurion astonished Jesus by his trust-faith. Is that a key to what you want in us, Jesus?

Demons knew more than people did about Jesus, calling him "Son of God." And demons obeyed Jesus' commands.

But when Jesus declared forgiveness, we might have agreed with the religious leaders that that was out of line for a human. However, Jesus backed his claim, showing his authority in the physical realm. Oh, now we see, he is more than a human! His appeal is to sinners. Great, we'll listen.

"God, please don't let anyone kill my body, for right now I am concerned about my soul. You ask that I love you more than my mother and father? If I receive you, I receive the one who sent you? God sent you? My response is not to turn away, for I do want rest for my soul."

"Who do you say I am?" Simon Peter answered, "You are the Christ, the Son of the living God. (Matthew 16:15–16. Chapters 12–16)

Matthew, you are telling us not to be surprised at this Jesus, for the role of servant is precisely what Isaiah (42:1–4) was directed by the Holy Spirit to write, six or seven centuries ago. Jesus not only did not submit to the earlier suggestions of Satan, but time and again overpowered the demons of Satan. Jesus, how can you die for three days only? Will I understand as I continue to read from this Book? What else will you do that is drastically different?

We have responsibility? We listen so that your words are not wasted. Your kingdom is of great value on an individual basis, not based upon language or ethnic group. We believe you are more than just the carpenter's son. We've come that far.

Matthew, thank you for recording all these events. Jesus miraculously fed thousands and walked on water! No wonder the crew worshiped Jesus and declared, "Truly, you are the Son of God."

Peter, you answered Jesus, speaking for yourself; and, likely, as typical representative of the disciples. Jesus is the Messiah (Hebrew language), the Christ (Greek language) and the Anointed One. We join others in worshiping Jesus.

This is my Son, whom I love; with Him I am well pleased. Listen to Him! (Matthew 17:5) *The Son of Man did not come to be served, but to serve, and to give his life as a ransom for many.* (20:28. Chapters 17–20)

Jesus stood and talked on earth as a human. He also did things man cannot do, only God. God even announced—gave his sanction—that Jesus was a special being, the only approved Son. (How can God have a son? Let's watch for further explanation later.) Then, Jesus has the characteristics of God, knows the will and mind of God, and correctly represents God to us three-dimensional people caught in time. How can one criticize what God fully approves and recommends to us? We dare not criticize; we dare to follow. (This is the second approval by God [3:17].) Yet, we seem so distant in following Jesus, especially considering the sermon Jesus gave on the hillside (Chapters 5–7).

Jesus was metamorphosed! Matthew was not talking about ghosts. The caterpillar-to-butterfly type of drastic change is an illustration; but Jesus changed back, apparently having more to say and do for us. Thank you.

Eternal life! That's a vital subject. Living by commandments, each of us fail; faith as a child and following, we'll try. Why would Jesus die and come alive? That seems strange for a god. The critical element is not in my life, but in Jesus. He gave his life as ransom. Even for each of us?

This is my blood of the covenant, which is poured out for many for the forgiveness of sins. (Matthew 26:28. Chapters 21:1–26:46)

Wow! All the TV networks would have been in Jerusalem interviewing Jesus and the people of the crowds. Many would be saying this Jesus was written about by the prophets. (See any footnotes in your Bible referring to Zechariah and the Psalms.) The people were exuberant.

Strange, isn't it, that Jesus rode a donkey—a servant's animal? Why wasn't he on a horse signifying military victory and regal power? Thinking of military, why hadn't Jesus chosen some disciples with military expertise?

Again, strange, instead of having conferences with religious leaders for teaching purposes, each meeting was a confrontation with the leaders wanting to kill him. They wanted to destroy the leader who had the possibility of establishing a new and desirous kingdom!

What else? A resurrection of people! The new kingdom will be for all people—all nations. There will be catastrophes and even an ending of this age. Jesus will return with an absolute control over all. He will convene courts and execute judgments!

Jesus, giving your lifeblood establishes a new covenant between man and God; then that replaces the lifeblood of animals (Leviticus 17:11). Accomplishment: atonement—covering of sins by Jesus. We want that. Wow!

What's next?

All authority in heaven and on earth has been given to me. Therefore go and make disciples of all nations....And surely I will be with you always, to the very end of the age. (Matthew 28:18–20. Chapters 26:47–28:20)

Judas, you stepped over the foul line. Sorry you did not repent instead of taking your life. What commotion—getting all the priests, religious leaders and government officials out of bed in the midst of the night. With all the meticulous protocols of the Hebrews and Romans, why all these illegal court sequences? If the public were watching the proceeding on TV, they would recognize these wrongs.

God, where are you? Aren't things out of control? Even Pilate seems to side with Jesus, yet loses control to the mob. People who, a few days before, had given praise now scream, "Crucify!" Jesus will die, for any person nailed in place for crucifixion dies. Jesus declines to call for angels!

Nature that had responded to Jesus' voice, now responds to Jesus' position on the cross with darkness, an earthquake, graves opening and the dead coming to life! Let's join the centurion, "Surely he was the Son of God!" Jesus died...Jesus comes to life! He said he would and did. And we're to tell others? Tell of Jesus' dying and rising for you and me? That is precisely what you said, Matthew, that Jesus would save people from their sins (1:21). Yes, Jesus!

Jesus...called to him those he wanted, and they came to him. He appointed twelve—designating them apostles.... (Mark 3:13–14. Chapters 1–3)

Jesus started to preach where he grew up, north of Jerusalem in Galilee. Jesus said there is good news, "Good news of God." He bid some fishermen to leave their occupation so they could be "fishers of men." What is that?

Religious leaders observed that Jesus taught with authority, rather different from the usual teachers. Evil spirits made another observation, "Jesus of Nazareth, you are the Holy One of God!" He bid spirits not to reveal his identity. Common people observed that Jesus was different, even forgiving sins as authenticated by his power in the physical realm.

Another day, as the religious leaders observed Jesus healing, they were infuriated because he did it (something considered work) on the Sabbath. From hence, religious groups united in their plot to kill Jesus.

Jesus appointed twelve to be his close disciples, to hear about "how to conduct yourself in daily living," and to observe day and night how this new religious leader himself lived. Jesus called them apostles: ones sent forth. Maybe these are fishers of men. Would we have been willing to leave our occupations after only a few weeks of observing this new religious leader who already had religious leaders in opposition? What else will Mark tell us about Jesus?

What's next, Mark?

They went out and preached that people should repent. (Mark 6:12. Chapters 4–6)

On the one hand, Jesus wanted followers to do God's will and receive the honorary title of "my brother and sister and mother." That would involve intent listening and thinking, "Let him hear." On the other hand, the new kingdom had aspects of which we do not understand.

Jesus calmed a storm as if speaking to a child, "Be quiet." He spoke to a legion of evil spirits as to a servant, "Move over." He did not need to speak to stop the blood flow of a woman. He brought a girl to life speaking as though she were napping, "Get up."

In the synagogue, all eyes were on Jesus. There were many positive reactions, and equally many negative ones. In the communities, Jesus taught and healed. The twelve disciples also healed, using their authority from Jesus. How many did Jesus feed? Five thousand men, plus women and children; shall we say more than 15,000? Everywhere, Jesus helped.

If I had been privileged to be a thirteenth disciple, would I have wondered about Jesus' goal? Was it to heal as many people as possible? To replace the present religious leadership? To be a fisher of men, I need to know clearly who/what I am selling. Is it you, Jesus? Yes. May all those people who are sorry for their sins, accept you.

"Who do you say I am?" Peter answered, "You are the Christ" (Mark 8:29). *For even the Son of Man...[came] to give his life as a ransom for many* (10:45. Chapters 7–10).

Yes, Jesus, we agree with the list of actions that come out of my heart. Can we be healed of these? Certainly, for Jesus healed a girl without going to the home to speak or touch her. He used his spit to heal a deaf and dumb man, fed 4,000 men and more by a miracle, and healed a man's blindness.

As "thirteenth disciple," each of us would have observed that none of the twelve left Jesus' side, none scoffed, none found Jesus' life sinful as theirs, all realized Jesus was more than man—like God!

Peter urged Jesus not to enter Jerusalem, knowing of the opposition. Would we have seconded the motion? Oops! Jesus did not take a vote, but severely rebuked Peter. Jesus' plan was to die and, in three days, rise to life! We would not have understood, "...Losing life to save it." Jesus will come sometime later in God's glory and establish a new kingdom.

Mark, you reiterate what Matthew noted: Jesus was metamorphosed. God said, "Listen to him." Jesus must somehow be God as well as human! The second time Jesus mentions rising, Peter keeps his mouth shut.

Yes, yes, we want eternal life. Is the kingdom of God and eternal life the same? For the third time, Jesus said he would die and rise; Jesus would die as a ransom. With Bartimaeus, we see, we see!

But, what's next?

Men will see the Son of Man coming in clouds with great power and glory (Mark 13:26). *Take it; this is my body....This is my blood of the covenant* (14:22–24. Chapters 11:1–14:42).

Mark agrees with Matthew that Jesus entered Jerusalem on a young donkey. The crowds certainly favored Jesus. He had many "home runs" with them by healing thousands. Yet, on the first day in Jerusalem, Jesus was in trouble; some wanting to kill him.

Jesus wants us to pray as though we were using a signed check with the amount left blank for us to enter! Ouch, but to do that we must have a clean slate of forgiving others.

Resurrection! You mean we were to have that assurance from the time of Moses? Then God is God of the ones who have died this earth's death, yet in his sight continue in some form of living.

Why will there be even more catastrophes between peoples? There already has been much war throughout history. The sky will be changed? He will return to gather his special people from all over the world? Jesus must be God to tell us about the future. As God, he will not need to apologize or retract any of his words. Much seems to be far in the future.

In the meantime, we will remember you, Jesus, using this bread to represent your body and this drink for your blood. Body and blood represent life! we're glad to bind ourselves to you, for you have this covenant that binds your life to mine.

My God, my God, why have you forsaken me? (Mark 15:34. Chapters 14:43–16:10; also Matthew 27:46)

Jesus clearly indicated to the high priest that there was a higher plan of God, that Jesus would go to the right hand of God and later return to earth. Pilate knew he was caught in a larger human scheme. We should say that all of them were within a vast plan—a plan of God!

Surrounding the cross, nature seemed to bow its head as though looking down in shame. Evil spirits had known that Jesus was God. Did nature now show that it knew? After being on the cross several hours, Jesus gave a loud cry. A dying human in excruciating pain and exhausting weakness would not have been able to call out, "My God, my God, why have you forsaken me?" David may well have felt that way (Psalm 22:1); Jesus meant it much more deeply. But God had announced he was pleased with Jesus as his Son. Now God removes his presence?

Jesus dies and is buried. Jesus rises and is living.

Then, God's forsaking was not because of Jesus' own life, but because of his association with our lives. The resurrection is our assurance that God has accepted that association, imputed our guilt to Jesus and, in reverse, imputed his righteousness to us. Impute: as a ship coming to port unloads one cargo and takes another.

Since Jesus did what he had announced several times—die and rise—we trust him. Hence, we trust Jesus' words that he will come again in great power and glory. There still is much we do not understand; that's part of trust. Come again, Jesus!

A Savior has been born to you; he is Christ the Lord. (Luke 2:11. Chapters 1–2)

Let's look at Jesus from Luke's record—the third biography. The birth of John the Baptist was miraculous. He was to be a herald for Jesus. The Holy Spirit caused Mary to conceive Jesus without any participation by a man! No wonder her child was called "Son of God." Somehow, Jesus was God and human at the same time. A Roman ruler called for a census, requiring Joseph and expectant Mary to travel to Bethlehem. Micah 5:2 says that someone special would be born there. Again, all these apparent coincidences were arranged by God, not man.

An angel went about town waking all the wealthy and ruling people. Wrong! An angel appeared to very commonplace working people—shepherds, saying, "A Savior is born!"

What was Mary treasuring in her heart? Her conception as a virgin and the purpose of her baby as told from the lips of the shepherds! A month later, Joseph and Mary were in the Temple mingling with other parents of babies one month old. Simeon held out his arms to Jesus and said, "My eyes have seen your salvation…to Gentiles…to Israel." Then Anna took Jesus and exclaimed, "Redeemer!" The Holy Spirit directed them to choose baby Jesus from among the many babies present.

Later, at his age of 12, the family was again at the Temple. Joseph and Mary were astonished at what Jesus said. No wonder Mary pondered. Wouldn't we?

I know who you are—the Holy One of God!...You are the Son of God! (Luke 4:34–41. Chapters 3–6)

Now it's interesting that Jesus did not bid tax collectors or soldiers to leave their occupations. Both occupations were despised by the Hebrews.

Matthew, Mark and Luke tell of the baptism and the uniqueness of God—Father, Son and Holy Spirit. All three writers told of the testing by Satan. Again, Jesus is no mere man. If we believe Jesus exists, then we must believe that Satan does, too. If Satan attacked Jesus with such intent, does he attack us in some manner?

The evil spirits surprise us. One called from a human body, "Have you come to destroy us?" They admitted Jesus had authority over them and were not bashful of telling Jesus' identity. The same day while healing many, several evil spirits shouted: "You are the Son of God!" Luke interprets that to mean that Jesus was the Christ—Messiah. That's the very person anticipated for centuries!

Jesus said good news would come by a new kingdom of God. Whatever the details, it would center upon himself.

Jesus showed control over disease and also authority to forgive sin. Common folk responded. But what is this? "Love your enemies....Do good....Bless....Forgive." How would Jesus expect us to apply all that?

He who rejects me rejects him who sent me....Rejoice that your names are written in heaven. (Luke 10:16, 20. Chapters 7–10)

What is all that mourning noise? A funeral. Jesus says to a corpse in a coffin, "Young man, get up." Any snickering, or was there silence? The dead man became alive and talked! The reaction: "God has come to help his people."

Jesus certainly helped a variety of people. To a sinful woman he declared forgiveness. He healed people from town after town. Upon being a little slow in responding to the synagogue ruler's daughter, she died. "She is not dead but asleep." Laughter! Jesus restores her to normal life. End of laughter.

At the transfiguration, God's voice was tender. Jesus is called Son. It was reassurance that Jesus was chosen by the Father. It was stern. I must listen.

Jesus encouraged the seventy (or seventy-two) he sent, saying, "He who rejects me rejects him who sent me." We don't want to believe in "some" god, but in the one who sent Jesus. We don't want to believe in a good man, but in Jesus whom God sent; in Christ (as Peter said), in God-Jesus. How is my name or yours written in heaven? Apparently by being close to the one who loves you—God. Similarly, that's what we say to a friend, "You're in my heart." Next?

Now one greater than Solomon is here...and now one greater than Jonah is here. (Luke 11:31–32. Chapters 11–14)

Why should Jesus speak of prayer so early in his ministry? Apparently, so we would use it. Each portion is awesome. We call God "Father." We will be careful with our lives in order to honor God's name. We want his kingdom and, in the meantime, want enough to sustain ourselves. God's forgiveness is contingent upon my forgiving others. Why? Premise: It is God's role to decide whom to forgive. Second premise: Since I am not God, I do not have that prerogative. Conclusion: I am to forgive others—period.

We are to ask, seek and knock; for God wants to give us the Holy Spirit. Luke or John, please explain the Holy Spirit further. And how strange that Jesus talked about returning but not about leaving.

Love it! The kingdom of God is like a great banquet. Some people on the guest list decline; many not expecting consideration, are invited. May we be in that group? We'll come! Question: why so severe—this "hating" kinfolk, carrying some kind of cross to follow Jesus and giving up everything? We try to listen.

Indeed, one greater than Solomon and Jonah is here. Jesus is greater in his own person; is greater with promises of the future; is greater with what is offered us; is greater in what he asks of us. I must read on.

No one who has left home or wife or brothers or parents or children for the sake of the kingdom of God will fail to receive many times as much in this age and, in the age to come, eternal life. (Luke 18:29–30. Chapters 15:1–19:27)

Someone in heaven watches decisions made here in this life, not matters prominent in the news about medical finds or warfare; but one's repentance and rejoices over such decisions. A person who is willing to declare himself inadequate in life and accepts the Savior creates a happy stir in heaven. Jesus said it twice!

We like this idea: Raise people from the dead and send them into town to talk. Abraham in heaven said, "NO, that we should hear [read] Moses and the prophets." But we think those risen would really get the attention of the public. Abraham said, "NO." We have to admit that people would still make excuses and rationalize. Instead of using extraordinary people, Jesus wants us ordinary people to do the witnessing.

The kingdom of God is within individual people. Then, that's how it can spread, for it's not limited to an ethnic or geographical group. Now we see, the key is: "God, have mercy on me, a sinner," and, "Receive the kingdom as a child." The benefit is: Eternal life!

But Jesus, those disciples left the income of their occupations and did not seem to be remunerated, let alone "many times over." Then, Jesus, you must mean we receive in other ways our quality of lifestyle now and, most certainly, eternal life later.

What's next, Luke?

Father, if you are willing, take this cup from me; yet not my will, but yours be done. (Luke 22:42. Chapters 19:28–22:65)

"Strange" isn't the best word; maybe "pathetic" is. The religious leadership wanted to kill Jesus. Common folk "hung on his words." Jesus is the key, the base, the king-pin, the cornerstone. Jesus made no bones about that. Your (my) conclusion is that this new kingdom hangs upon the person of Jesus Christ! YES or NO?

Yes, there will be a resurrection in order to enter God's presence. There is no return to this earth in another personalization, nor a second chance. The resurrected ones will "no longer die." They "are like angels" and "are God's children."

The bad news is that calamities will surround Jerusalem. The good news is that those events portend the return of Jesus Christ with power and glory!

Satan influenced Judas. Won't he leave God's people alone? No, for that's the nature of the Beast. Once, when Satan attacked Peter, Jesus prayed for him.

A king's cup could contain the best wine or the poison of death. Often a slave was to drink from the cup ahead of the king, testing it with his life. Jesus knew his cup represented the poison of death. Isaiah had said (51:22) there would be a moment when God would pour out his wrath in a cup. Here was God's wrath against sin, our sin, your sin, my sin. "Yet not my will, but yours be done." Knowing what lie ahead, yet he would go. What love!

Father, forgive them, for they do not know what they are doing (Luke 23:34). *Today you will be with me in paradise* (23:43). *Father, into your hands I commit my spirit* (23:46. Chapters 22:66–23:49).

They whisked Jesus before religious leaders by means of illegal proceedings. "Are you the Christ?" Affirmative. "Are you the Son of God?" Affirmative. Bedlam! Their premise: Jesus was only a man. Second premise: Jesus had assumed the role of God. Conclusion: Blasphemy. Prescription: Death.

This cup of God's wrath apparently would be carried out by God's sovereignty working through human circumstances. Pilate lost control. Jesus was sent for crucifixion. Crucifixion, we are told, is the most painful way to die. Listen to the noisy scoffing. They should shut up and listen, for Jesus has more to say.

"Father, forgive...." Jesus had said to us, "Love your enemies, pray for them." He did! Jesus could have cursed them, blinded, killed, or called angels. He prayed for them. Thank you, Jesus, you did what you bid us to do. "Today...in paradise." That man was not baptized, did not receive communion, did not memorize any liturgy, nor spoke in tongues; yet, he went from here to Paradise! Hurrah! "Father, into your hands...." Jesus finished his "day" and, instead of resigning himself to death, committed himself to God, the Father.

What happened next, Luke?

The Christ will suffer and rise from the dead on the third day, and repentance and forgiveness of sins will be preached in his name to all nations. (Luke 24:46–47. Chapters 23:50–24:53)

Just after the Hebrew Sabbath, two women looked for the body of Jesus at the tomb. Gone. Two men—angels—spoke, "Remember how he told you...on the third day be raised again." Yes, Jesus had said this over and over. The women hurried back to the disciples. Nonsense...Peter checked for himself....True!

How tender. Two people (no mention of gender) walking, and Jesus steps alongside. They were kept from recognizing him. They tell of reports that Jesus' body is missing. Jesus talks of the Christ, the Messiah, using all the Scriptures. (To us, that's the Old Testament.) Finally, upon their sharing hospitality, "Their eyes were opened."

Jesus appeared that same day to the eleven and others. He illustrated how that it was he, "Everything must be fulfilled that is written about me in the Law of Moses, the Prophets and the Psalms." Jesus opened their minds so that they could understand on the basis of Scripture. Because of his death and rising, we now have the message of repentance and forgiveness of sins for ALL nations.

All this is exactly what Luke said he would write for us. Thank you, Luke, for giving an orderly account of things fulfilled as told by eyewitnesses. We believe in Jesus.

CONVERSATIONAL PRAYER

This is a good place to pause, after reading Matthew, Mark and Luke. We'll separate John because it was written nearly a half-century later. When we say that we know Tom or Betty, that does not mean that we know all the details of one's life, but it does mean that we understand significant actions and intentions of that person. May we tell God that we know Jesus Christ, his intentions for being here on earth and dying to benefit us.

God, I didn't know what kind of a savior and kingdom to look for. Jesus, you said to be sorry for things in my life and that you had good news about a new kingdom. It seems you are not looking for letters of recommendation from my friends, nor for my latest resume. You want me to be sorry. I'm not as good as I often think I am. Yet, you want me to lead a very idyllic life. I'll never be able to work up to that. Then you made clear the idea of a ransom by means of a savior who pays with his life in my place. That's you, Jesus. I have no grounds for asking you to be my substitute, but now I know that's what you intended to do all along. Sometimes I think I would have caught on quicker than the disciples—but I suppose not. Now I realize that you, Jesus, gave us enough evidence to know that you were, and are, God. In childlike trust, I believe. And with the same desire as the one on the other cross, I want to enter your Paradise when I leave this life. I'll try to live more as you want. Jesus, you talked about and demonstrated such a high standard. Will there be any other assistance for that?

(May you express yourself in prayer using your vocabulary and style.)

FOURTH
BIOGRAPHY

Word...Son...Lamb...Messiah. (John 1:1, 18, 29, 41. Chapter 1)

For the fourth time, we have a biography that will help us consider who Jesus is.

Skipping details of human birth, John goes back to the beginning—meaning prior to this world. John says that God's communication is by a person who was and is God, and is appropriately called the "Word." The emphasis is on God speaking, commanding, communicating. This is different than atomic and chemical powers gradually and continuously at work. But John personalizes this "mover" by using the word "Word" as a part of God. This Word-God part shared with the rest of God in creating.

All people who believe in this Word receive the title of "Children of God," apart from what their human lineage might be. Amazing. This Word took a human form and became Christ Jesus. He is distinctively and uniquely the Son of God, since it was the Holy Spirit who caused the virgin Mary to conceive. But, also, Jesus Christ has seen God since he was with God, was God and is God.

John the Baptist was descriptive, "Look, the Lamb of God, who takes away the sin of the world!" Had we been Hebrew persons offering an animal day after day for sins (Leviticus 17:11), we would likely have rebelled because an animal is beneath our dignity as humans. Now, realizing that Jesus is above our dignity, we can agree with John the Baptist—here is our Lamb.

Andrew agreed and hurried to his brother Simon [Peter], saying, "We have found the Messiah," the Christ, the Anointed One. Also, Philip said, "We have found the one Moses wrote about." The one Moses and the prophets wanted to meet, their desire over the centuries, is revealed in the person Jesus Christ!

Whoever believes in the son has eternal life, but whoever rejects the son will not see life, for God's wrath remains on him. (John 3:36. Chapters 2–3)

Jesus changed water into wine. Just to save embarrassment for the host? No, to reveal his glory; to affirm the person John introduces in his opening paragraphs.

Next in significance, Jesus stepped into the Temple courtyard at holy Passover time and scattered the profiteers. Worship had been exchanged for profit. By what authority did he do this? By the authority behind the power that he would allow himself to be "destroyed" and yet be restored in three days. Restore the Temple building? No, his body.

Now here is a good man, a very good man, Nicodemus. He would not see the kingdom nor enter it? That's like popping a guy's balloon. Nicodemus needs a new life by the Spirit. That's such a change that Jesus calls it being "born again," or "born from above." He illustrates by referring to the bronze snake Moses made (Numbers 21). Then, each person who looked to God's provision outside one's own life, received life (continued physical life at that time). Now, each one who looks beyond one's self to God's provision in Jesus—the Son of Man lifted up for attention— receives eternal life!

As we believe in Jesus, we are not condemned by Holy God. If we do not believe in this provision, we are condemned primarily because of rejecting the offer. Rejecting brings God's wrath. We cannot bargain.

Whoever hears my word and believes him who sent me has eternal life and will not be condemned; he has crossed over from death to life. (John 5:24. Chapters 4–5)

Jesus speaks with a Samaritan woman and offers help that would bring eternal life. She counters that such help would only come from the Messiah (called Christ). "I am he." As the people of her town listen to Jesus, they believe that he is "the Savior of the world."

For a royal official, Jesus healed his son even though miles distant. Upon arriving home, the father talked of Jesus. He and his household believed.

Jesus spoke to a man, invalid 38 years, "Get up!" He did, whole.

Jesus did such "work" on the Sabbath. The religious leaders wanted to kill him, especially because he called God his Father. That implied he claimed he was God. They correctly understood Jesus' teaching, for he said it another way, "He who does not honor the Son does not honor the Father, who sent him." Then, believing that Jesus is the one he claims to be is the key. The benefit—actually, a gift—is eternal life and release from condemnation. Jesus says it differently: The benefit is to cross over from death, the condemnation, to life. To alive people, Jesus explains that one can anticipate eternal life or eternal death. The purpose for Jesus was, as he said to the Samaritan woman, "To finish his [God's] work." He knew it and announced it.

What's next, John?

For my Father's will is that everyone who looks to the son and believes in him shall have eternal life, and I will raise him up at the last day. (John 6:40. Chapters 6–9)

Apparently, many people of good intentions wanted to make Jesus king. He withdrew. Others asked sincerely what God requires. "Believe in the one he has sent." How would they recognize such a one? Believe in the Son—him—and have eternal life? Precisely what Jesus declares, he grants, for he came from heaven.

Some followers left Jesus, but not Peter. "You have the words of eternal life. We believe and know that you are the Holy One of God." Yet there was another aspect of his life for which the time was not right (first said at 2:4). Again, amidst conflict, Jesus repeated this twice (7:30; 8:20). While still in Jerusalem, he declared very publicly that people are to believe in him in order to have the Spirit, though later. Maybe John will tell us more about the Holy Spirit.

John shows that Jesus was specific about himself. "I told you that you would die in your sins; if you do not believe that I am the one I claim to be..." (8:24). "For I came from God and now am here." Jesus' response to some who were complaining: "I Am" (8:58). That's the same title God used in speaking to Moses! (Exodus 3:14).

John next gives the healing of a man blind from birth. Jesus used this to illustrate spiritual blindness. Then the man had both kinds of sight!

I am the bread of life (John 6:35). *I am the light of the world* (8:12, 9:5). *I am the gate* (10:9). *I am the good shepherd* (10:11). *I am the resurrection and the life* (11:25). *I am the way and the truth and the life* (14:6). *I am the true vine* (15:1).

BREAD: Bread is a staple food in any society, a necessity. Jesus likens his body to bread, in particular to the manna (Exodus 16) which miraculously came from heaven. Likewise, Jesus is from heaven. You and I must "eat," "partake" of him.

LIGHT: Jesus gives "light" to one's life. Jesus illustrated that we need guidance by giving a blind man his sight.

GATE [DOOR], SHEPHERD: There is one gate into the sheepfold; Jesus is the entryway for our security. A good shepherd guides but also is willing to lay down his life for the sheep (Reread Psalm 23).

RESURRECTION—LIFE: Matthew, Mark and Luke told us Jesus was resurrected. Hence he can make this offer to us and NO ONE else can. He does. "I, (your name), believing in Jesus, will live even though I, (your name), will die bodily." With Martha: "Yes!"

WAY—TRUTH—LIFE: Jesus is the way to God's presence, is the only true message, and is the means of eternal life. "NO ONE comes to the Father except through me."

VINE: There's more than banner waving; there is to be a lifestyle and fruitbearing. Close fellowship, day after day, gives us help.

Lazarus, come out! (John 11:43. Chapters 10:1–12:11)

Sheep are sensitive to one's voice. They will scatter at the voice of a stranger, but come at the voice of their shepherd. We, likewise, are to recognize Jesus and follow him. Does Jesus need to lay down his life? Human circumstances seem to force this event, but it will be by Jesus' willingness to exercise such power. More is involved; dying and rising is the plan or command of God the Father! (10:18). Strange.

Some people did not benefit from all the explanations. (At this point, we could have a discussion of human responsibility and God's sovereignty.) To those who do believe, Jesus gives eternal life. They shall never perish; no one can snatch them away. All this because Jesus and the Father are one! Jesus pleaded with the other people but never forced them.

Lazarus, a close friend, was sick. Jesus would use that occasion to bring glory to himself. Jesus lingered; Lazarus died. Jesus said he would go and awaken him from death. He prefaced his action by prayer, "That they may believe that you sent me....Lazarus, come out!" He did! That brought glory to Jesus. Will it be that simple for Jesus to call us by name at the future resurrection? Ironically, now some wanted to kill both of them.

Mary poured expensive perfume on Jesus' feet. She meant it in love and praise. Jesus said it was to be considered a symbol of his burial.

Peace I leave with you; my peace I give you...do not be afraid. (John 14:27. Chapters 12:12–16:33)

John, too, describes the entry of Jesus into Jerusalem. All four Gospels give about one-third of their space to one week in the life of Jesus. The birth week? No. The death week! Ah, there's the significance of these events. Now his hour, or time, has come to be glorified. Happy time? Not really. Time to face death. Look, the battle is engaged again between Jesus and Satan. Jesus will drive Satan back and there will be a big win on Jesus' part. Some people still could not believe, just as Isaiah warned (53:1).

Satan provokes Judas to turn against Jesus. Jesus predicts the betrayal. Jesus also predicts Peter's three-time denial.

Jesus gives the command that we love one another. That is new. Jesus did that himself, and he expects it of us. That is to be a primary characteristic of believers; so much so, that nonbelievers will observe this love.

Now, Jesus talks of his leaving—going to prepare a place for us. Then he will return to get us and take us with him. Hurrah!

Jesus explains that we have help by the Holy Spirit. He will be your Comforter and will teach things Jesus has said. Be glad that Jesus has left, for he was only in one place at a time, whereas the Holy Spirit is in believers wherever they are. Now I understand a little about the Holy Spirit. We have peace differently than what the world offers.

Now this is eternal life: that they may know you, the only true God, and Jesus Christ whom you have sent. (John 17:3. Chapters 17–19)

Jesus prays that God, the Father, may glorify him. Is Jesus to become king? Some people hoped so, based upon the Old Testament. No, Jesus makes it clear that his goal on earth is to present eternal life. This is given to each one who knows, believes, and trusts God and Jesus Christ. May Jesus return to the glory he had prior to this world. May those who have come to believe be protected by the power in God's name and in Jesus' name, and protected from the evil one—Satan. Satan is expected to continue in battle with humans regarding their allegiance. Throughout generations, believing ones will have a sense of unity with Jesus and with one another that amazes the other people of the world.

False arrest, illegal trials, questions. A cruel switch: Barabbas for Jesus. Jesus prayed to be glorified. That sign: "Jesus of Nazareth, the King of the Jews," some thought it was mockery, others thought it was glorious.

But listen, Jesus speaks, "Woman...Son....Mother." Instead of vitriolic talk, he speaks love. Instead of self-pity, he wills good for his survivors. All the human anger and jealousy at the scene can't stop that. "I thirst." He is human—no apparition on the cross. He is clear in his mind; is not a stoic. "It is finished." Craftsmen can stand back after long hours of work and say, "It is finished." In three years of public view, Jesus finished what he intended; yea, what God the Father intended. The Greek word "finished" emphasizes perfection—absolute completeness.

Is this the end? What's next?

But these are written that you may believe that Jesus is the Christ, the Son of God, and that by believing you may have life in his name. (John 20:31. Chapters 20–21)

Witnesses, give your reports. The stone had been moved from in front of the tomb. By whom? The body of Jesus is gone! Who took it? Burial clothes were still there, some neatly aside. How so? Peter and John (he was the other disciple) looked and went home. Mary, crying, saw two angels. Jesus called her by name. He had to go to God, our Father. She was to tell others and she did.

And you disciples? Jesus appeared to us that evening. We had locked the doors of the hall, but Jesus appeared! Thomas missed that meeting, but said he wanted to see evidences that this Jesus was the one who had been on the cross; a week later, he did see.

Anything happen after that? Oh yes, the disciples went fishing. All night long they caught nothing. Someone on shore recommended simply moving the net to the other side of the boat. Ha, they had a huge catch! John said to Peter, "It is the Lord." Ashore, Jesus already had fish and bread cooked. He took Peter aside and tenderly, but firmly, recommissioned him. Peter needed that.

John's report: "Jesus did many other miraculous signs in the presence of his disciples, which are not recorded in this book. But these are written that you may believe that JESUS IS THE CHRIST, the Son of God, and that by believing you may have LIFE IN HIS NAME."

Let's make our report: We believe and cry for joy!

CONVERSATIONAL PRAYER

John, writing some years later, finds there is still no fault to present; no reason to discredit Jesus as the one prophesied to be both man and God. How shall we pray?

Jesus, I don't understand how you existed prior to this world, or could be human and God at the same time. I see your purpose is to communicate God to us, be the message—WORD. I believe you died in my place to give me eternal life as a gift prepaid by your death. I see now in a small way the battle between Satan and you, and that Satan can struggle with me, too. As I see from these Gospels how easily people let jealousies and biases hinder a relationship with you, I have to admit I might have that problem, too. Thank you for leaving the earth and giving in your place the Holy Spirit who came into my life when I believed. No wonder you said there would be a new kingdom, for it is not bound geographically. Thank you, Holy Spirit, for guiding as to what was recorded in Scriptures so I could believe. Now, please continue to teach and guide me.

(May you express yourself in prayer using your words.

Note: We observe that the Gospels are not a day-by-day journal attempting to record all things said and done by Jesus and the disciples. Each Gospel writer intentionally selected certain events in order to emphasize the person and purpose of Jesus. They do not need to agree as to which items to include. Each writer used vocabulary and writing styles—evident in studying the Greek originals—in accord with his personality and different cultural background. Even one was from a doctor's view. The Holy Spirit had an overarching control of these biographies.)

ACTS AND ROMANS

He was taken up before their very eyes, and a cloud hid him from their sight. (Acts 1:9. Chapter 1)

Act II, Scene II: The Followers

We dream of the equipment Buck Rogers used or that Star Wars had, but we're really not expecting to see a person rise from the ground and disappear beyond the clouds. A balloon, yes; a person, no. Jesus did!

Jesus changed the conversation from that of the kingdom of Israel to that of witnessing. To what will we witness? What we first learned from Matthew, Mark, Luke and John: that he was and still is God. He died on purpose to pay with his life for our sin-prone nature. He was resurrected, which shows the acceptance by the Godhead and gives us the assurance that there is a resurrection for those who follow. A kingdom has begun that cuts across social and ethnic lines, and Jesus will finalize this when he returns in great glory. Jesus gives love, joy, peace and purpose to this earthly life. All this is indeed good news!

To whom are we to speak? Jesus outlined the program: Go to one's locale, then to the adjoining country and, without stopping, to all the earth.

Nineteen centuries have passed. Have the believers done this? Fairly well. Are we done? No! Wycliffe Bible Translators and the many Bible societies tell us there are hundreds of languages into which we should translate at least the New Testament.

Jesus, you left; but thanks for leaving the Holy Spirit to be with us, our Helper in daily living and in sharing with others.

And you will receive the gift of the Holy Spirit. The promise is for you and your children and..." (Acts 2:38–39. Chapter 2)

The apostles gathered in a home on the special festival day, Pentecost. Suddenly there was a loud "wind" sound, tongue-shaped "fire" landed on each person, and they spoke in other languages! Luke, the author, says that was the Holy Spirit coming upon them. Jews who had traveled from many countries for Pentecost heard this "wind." Crowds gathered. These visiting Jews would have understood the local Greek or Aramaic, but they heard these apostles speaking in the languages of their home countries. They spoke of the wonders of God. Amazing!

Often there is a spoilsport in a crowd. There was, and he suggested the speakers were drunk. Heeeere's Peter! He explained that all this was the completion of the message Joel had given a few hundred years before. In the Greek language, the same word is used for *wind* as for *spirit*. This was not a physical wind, but the Holy Spirit. Peter continued with a sermon as to God's purpose, overriding all the human conflict surrounding Jesus. The resurrection was even foretold in Psalms by David.

What is one to do about all this? Be sorry for the ways we are short in pleasing God (sins), declare our trust in Jesus Christ and receive the Holy Spirit. That was a recommendation to the people then, and it is a promise down to our generation today!

What's next will be made clear.

Salvation is found in no one else, for there is no other name under heaven given to men by which we must be saved. (Acts 4:12. Chapters 3–4)

Peter preached again that God raised Jesus from death, or from among the dead ones, and that one should repent. Jesus Christ has gone to heaven and will remain there until a special event in the future. In the meantime, all people—Jew and non-Jew (Gentile)—are to be blessed by this message in Jesus Christ.

Trouble again—the Sadducees did not believe in any resurrection. (Hence, a play on the name, for they were sad-you-see.) They were greatly disturbed, for this new message from the disciples centered upon the resurrection of Jesus and the confidence that believers had of the coming resurrection. Hence, the bottom line from the lips of Peter, "There is no other name...to be saved."

Conflict was at a climax as the religious leaders told Peter and John not to speak of Jesus. That would be disobeying God, for they "cannot help speaking what we have seen and heard." Upon being released and returning to their friends, prayer went up like an aroma, and power came down and shook the place.

"With great power the apostles continued to testify to the resurrection of the Lord Jesus...."

I see heaven open and the Son of Man standing at the right hand of God. (Acts 7:56. Chapters 5–7)

As we know, sometimes bad things happen to good people. Stephen was a good man, one of seven especially "full of the Spirit and wisdom." Stephen did wonders and miracles beyond the others. Opposition arose from Jewish leaders in outlying areas to the north and south. They sought false witnesses against Stephen. The leaders saw his face unusually different, "...Like an angel" (6:15).

Then it was Stephen's turn to speak. He reviewed how God had intervened in personal lives and in the nation many times. As far back as Moses, there was the assurance that a Special Person was to come. Even Amos and Isaiah had made comments applicable to Jesus.

Now the leaders were furious. Stephen was ecstatic because he saw Jesus at the right hand of God, and said so. They were more infuriated and dragged him out of the city to stone him, for killing was not allowed in the city. But listen, for he, like Jesus, had last words: "Lord Jesus, receive my spirit." His prayer was to, or through, Jesus Christ, as Jesus taught. "Lord, do not hold this sin against them." In fact, Stephen died. In pictorial form, he fell asleep. That implies that sometime he will awaken.

Off to the side, a man—Saul—watched with approval.

Who are you, Lord? (Acts 9:5. Chapters 8–9)

God, you just used Philip to help the Ethiopian officer believe in Jesus, based upon the written Scripture. Now, God, you've let this fellow, Saul, who had approved of Stephen's death, wreak havoc with several thousand believers in and near Jerusalem. What were the disciples to do?

God did the doing. God stopped Saul, spoke to him and blinded him! Poor guy, I would not have prayed for that to happen. God called Ananias to go across town to meet Saul. Why him? To pray for him; he's chosen to be instrumental in speaking to Gentiles. Ananias went and Saul was released from the blindness and was baptized.

Saul stayed in Damascus several days in order to be with the disciples, not to oppose them. Now, as he told from day to day in synagogues that Jesus is the Son of God, the Jews wanted to kill him.

What a turnabout for Saul. He was stopped from doing one thing and "held" by blindness a while. Then he was redirected by listening to the main body of disciples, receiving a crash course in the new Christian message. Now he could answer his question: "Who are you, Lord?" Answer: Jesus is the Christ, the one promised throughout the Old Testament.

What is the significant work ahead for Saul? What's next, Luke? (Luke, the Gospel writer, wrote Acts.)

He commanded us to preach to the people and to testify that he is the one whom God appointed...that everyone who believes in him receives forgiveness of sins through his name. (Acts 10:42–43. Chapters 10–12)

Peter had been recommissioned by Jesus. He had already been preaching and handling the opposition. Peter was "successful." Yet, God wanted Peter's attention. Choosing noon one day when he was hungry, God presented a vision of a sheet on which were many varieties of animals. God directed, "Kill and eat."

Thinking of the Jewish laws based upon the Old Testament which said that certain animals were not to be eaten, Peter retorted that he had been obedient to what he had been taught and should not eat from this variety. God spoke again, declaring all animals "clean" (edible). A third time God presented this thought; then the vision was gone. We wonder if Peter reflected upon his triple denial of Jesus and upon Jesus' threefold commission?

Cornelius was a Roman officer, a leader of a hundred military men. He and his family were religious—worshiping and praying to God regularly, even giving to the poor. One afternoon he received a vision. An angel bid him to send to Joppa (30 miles south) for Simon Peter. Without dispute or delay, he sent for him. Peter arrived to find Cornelius' house filled with a crowd! Peter caught on: the "variety" is Jew and Gentile. The message of Jesus Christ is for all people of all generations, "That everyone who believes in him receives forgiveness of sins...." Soon, believers were called Christians (11:26).

Believe in the Lord Jesus, and you will be saved—you and your household. (Acts 16:31. Chapters 13–20)

Paul had gone on a missionary journey (13:1ff), and started a second journey (15:36ff). People's lives had been changed by the emphasis upon Christ's resurrection and, hence, by the confidence we have in our future resurrection.

Uh-oh, selfishness on the part of money makers caused Paul and Silas to be arrested, beaten, and placed in a security cell. How would this end? Did Paul and Silas whine and solicit pity from other inmates? Did they raise their fists in anger? NO. At midnight, they sang and prayed to God. Other prisoners could not help but hear, likely also the jailkeeper.

An earthquake! Prison doors were jarred open, and leg and arm chains fell out of the walls. The jailkeeper rushed over and, supposing prisoners had escaped, drew his sword to kill himself. Why wait for the death sentence from the court martial the next day? "Stop, we are all here!" With lanterns, he verified Paul's words to his great relief.

No wonder the jailer fell before Paul and Silas. He was trembling because his life was safe. He knew that Paul and Silas were a different "breed of cat." These two knew God. How, then, could he be saved from his life of intrigue and false accusations, to know a different life with God? The jailer and his family believed and were baptized that night! Paul and Silas were escorted out. The end.

I pray God that not only you but all who are listening to me today may become what I am.... (Acts 26:29. Chapters 21–28)

This time, Paul, having been arrested, was before Festus, a Roman governor. Visitor King Agrippa and his sister Bernice arrived. He was a provincial king and each, Festus and Agrippa, solicited the favor of the other. In the midst of pomp, elegant clothing and thrones surrounded by many dignitaries in their finest regalia—in stark contrast—stood Paul, in chains in the middle of the great hall. Agrippa to Paul: "Speak."

Paul, respectful of those present, told of his upbringing and vigorous loyalty to the Jewish message; hence, his opposition to the new message of Jesus. However, God changed him and sent him to support this message of forgiveness and cleansing life in Jesus Christ, available even for the Gentiles. This message is based upon promises Jews found in Moses and the prophets—that an anointed One would come, suffer (die) and rise from the dead for Jews and for Gentiles.

Festus interrupted. Paul continued to appeal for the mind and conscience of Agrippa. "Do you believe the prophets?"

Implied answer: "Yes."

"Become a Christian."

Implied: "No." Agrippa closed the meeting.

Paul ignored any disdain and spoke to all those standing in the hall then, and to us living today as well. "I pray to God…" that each one knows forgiveness and looks forward to the resurrection. Our response?

For since the creation of the world God's invisible qualities—his eternal power and divine nature—have been clearly seen…so that men are without excuse. (Romans 1:20. Chapter 1)

Paul traveled northward through many lands making three trips as a traveling preacher. He described himself as a "servant of Christ Jesus" and "an apostle and set apart for the gospel of God." Toward the end of his third trip, while in Corinth, he wrote this letter to believers in Rome. He wished them grace and peace that comes from a relationship with Jesus Christ as Lord and director of life. He gave thanks for them and prayed for them.

He becomes serious, for there is another kind of life, one of intentionally ignoring God. Today, one might say, "I want to do my own thing." Such people don't give God any value nor thank him for this life. Then occurs a horrible sequence. God allows a kind of living which grows more and more self-centered: sexual wrongs, twisting truth and falsehood, serving and even worshiping created things instead of the Creator. He gives a list of a dozen acts and thought patterns that are symptoms of a life without God; placing "I" as the god. Then, what conscience remains is numbed. Such a person does these and seeks others who also do the same. Horrors.

When does one make the decision as to which life to have? Paul places that moment back at one's perception of the world, for creation exhibits God with an indescribable power and nature. You and I are without excuse, if this view of God is denied.

To be just and the one who justifies the man who has faith in Jesus. (Romans 3:26. Chapters 2–3)

You are so careful to hold us to the point, Paul. All…all have sinned and come short of what God would like in our lives. Then, if everyone has this problem of not pleasing God, why worry? Various societies have various rules. Are some better than others? Uh-oh, Paul says none will be considered righteous by God for observing laws. Instead, laws really make us "conscious of sin!" Then, since we need help, where do we turn?

There is a righteousness that God has made known. Where,…how? It centers in faith—trust in Christ Jesus. We must believe that God has arranged an acceptable relationship by Christ Jesus. There is absolutely no difference among us, since we all—Jew or non-Jew, any nationality, or any skin color—have the serious problem of being short of what God wants in our lives. We all have a sin-prone nature. The good news is that there is a redemption—a change of status in God's evaluation of us by means of Christ Jesus! How? God arranged that Christ would be an atonement (remember the animal sacrifice in the Old Testament), that he would overcome God's righteous wrath. I am to believe Christ Jesus gave his life for me!

In a sense, sins under the Old Testament were not fully covered by animal sacrifice, for animals were beneath the dignity of people. Full coverage awaited Jesus. The sacrifice of Jesus, not being simply equal to my dignity but above my dignity, is completely adequate. God is just and cannot overlook wrong; however, he justifies—declares just—you and me the moment we trust his method, believing in Christ Jesus. Great! What's next, Paul?

153

Therefore, since we have been justified through faith, we have peace with God through our Lord Jesus Christ. (Romans 5:1. Chapters 4–5)

Often we talk about access to the computer file, to the bank account, to the boss, etc. Does the believer have access to Holy God? Yes, by this faith Paul has described. The arrangement is more than legal; it is that, and is also gracious. God was not obliged to do as he did, but did so out of love. Paul uses the word "grace." We picture grace as: <u>G</u>od's <u>R</u>iches <u>A</u>t <u>C</u>hrist's <u>E</u>xpense. Indeed, it is at the expense of his life. Paul had just said, "He was delivered over to death for our sins and was raised to life for our justification" (4:25).

In addition, there is peace with God. Peace is often declared after cessation of war. Peace with God has meaning after considering the wrath of God. We have glimpses of God's wrath from the Old Testament and as we look at the Cross. We are released from the wrath of God and have peace with God by what Jesus accomplished.

Believing is made clear. It is not simply believing that Jesus was a good person, a miracle worker or an example as a martyr. It is believing Jesus is what he said he was—God; and believing Jesus did what he said he would—lay down his life and rise again for our benefit. Believing is trusting this method made known by God as the only way to be acceptable to Holy God! All by G-R-A-C-E.

What a wretched man I am! Who will rescue me from this body of death? (Romans 7:24. Chapters 6–7)

Apparently this life, even for the believer, is not just "pie in the sky," nor is it always lilacs and roses. As we listen to the news media reporting on the world or on the neighborhood, we realize much goes wrong.

Paul seems to hang outdoors all of his "dirty clothes" for anyone to see. He has been successful at giving the message of Jesus in a multitude of cities and regions. He is respected by other leaders. Aren't you perfect, Paul? "No." There is an awful conflict inside. Is Paul sick? No, He is human. In every believer there are two tendencies, two natures. One is trying to listen to God and to please him; the other nature wants to do wrong, which is symptomatic of the sin-prone nature within.

In a way, life was simpler before becoming a believer. Then there was one goal—to serve self, including whatever way Satan would suggest. But the believer has an additional modus operandi: striving to please God. The two natures, being vastly different (in fact, opposites), create an ongoing conflict. I remember a man I considered to be a believer who was often drunk. He had a terrible time with this conflict.

Apparently Paul was often weary of this conflict. He could at least be honest in his admission. He claims help in this life by Jesus Christ as director of life. He claims complete release later when this earthly body is finished!

Since we are not likely any better than Paul, we, too, won't have complete release until this life is finished.

What, then, shall we say in response to this? If God is for us, who can be against us? (Romans 8:31. Chapters 8–11)

How wonderful that the Holy Spirit intercedes for us. An intercessor often says things in private. Likewise, we can't understand just how this help of the Spirit takes place; but we do give thanks for it.

Paul claims that in the midst of all incidents in life, God works some good for each one who loves him! This is a big subject that should be given time and many words with great patience and tenderness. I have experienced the loss of a loved one, my wife. What grief is yours? God works good? An illustration often used is the appearance of a weaving. On one side it is a miscellaneous, even tangled, mesh of threads and color; on the other side is a beautiful pattern. Can we accept that God's pattern is to work beautifully together those characteristics Paul already mentioned: perseverance, character, hope, and a renewed sense of God's love? (5:3–5). More than that, for God foreknows (somehow), predestines (somehow) us to work toward some likeness of his Son. The believer is called, justified and glorified!

Our response? Rejoice, for "If God is for us, who can be against us?" Christ completed the arrangements on earth and now intercedes in heaven for us. A further exultation for us: we are "More than conquerors!" What worth I have! How I give thanks for myself! I'm ready to live today. No incident will separate me from the powerful love God has for me.

Therefore, I urge you, brothers [men and women believers], in view of God's mercy, to offer your bodies as living sacrifices, holy and pleasing to God—which is your spiritual worship. (Romans 12:1. Chapters 12–15)

Story: I was floundering, unable to swim, so close to drowning, and cried for help. Seemingly at the last moment, someone rescued me. He had the strength and character to do so. I appreciated that at the time, but even more so later when I heard further details and met the one who rescued me.

So, in appreciation, I brought a gift. It was not an item bought in a store, but something of myself that I made. As I presented it, I did not say, "I am young and intelligent and deserved to be rescued." Nor, "I give this to you to pay for your time and trouble," as though to earn my rescue. I said, "Thank you, I am undeserving. I give this simply in appreciation." Like Paul, now we, brothers and sisters in Christ, can see the difference between earning and appreciating.

Therefore, understanding the rescue that Christ has performed and acknowledging that I am undeserving, what then can I do, what can I give? In appreciation, give something of yourself, offer your whole self as a daily living sacrifice. Jesus was our dying sacrifice. We need to struggle not to conform to the pattern of living as generally portrayed in the news media. Instead, be transformed—energized, focused, empowered—by a new mindset or goal; that of seeking God's will and finding it to be "his good, pleasing and perfect will."

Gospel…revealed…so that all nations might believe and obey him—to the only wise God be glory forever through Jesus Christ! Amen. (Romans 16:26–27. Chapter 16)

How can one summarize all that Paul has written? Paul's life was jerked by God from one goal of opposing the Way, to the opposite goal of preaching salvation by none other than Christ. He went at first to Jews, but later devoted himself to Gentiles. He experienced hardship and could speak from a life subjected to injustices. God used him to write with clarity, conciseness and conviction, "I am not ashamed of the gospel, because it is the power of God for the salvation of everyone who believes: first for the Jew, then for the Gentile" (1:16). He sits in one city, Corinth, and writes to believers in Rome.

Anything different in humanity between Corinth and Rome? No. Between those in San Antonio and Seattle? No. There is the same dastardly problem—sin. There is the same solution—not earning one's way, but accepting God's righteousness freely offered in Christ Jesus. There is the same goal—offering one's life in gratitude to be as pleasing as possible to God, and then anticipating the future resurrection.

Paul closes as though writing his epitaph. What would you write for yourself? You have heard the emphasis at some funerals: "He had lots of big boy's toys," or, "He was rich." In contrast, have you heard: "He believed Jesus," or, "She sacrificed much to please Jesus"? This gospel is revealed (not developed by man) so that people of any nation might believe and obey.

With Paul: "Amen!"

CONVERSATIONAL PRAYER

Having read Acts and Romans, what should we pray?

Jesus, you left the earth; but thank you for leaving the Holy Spirit here in your place and gathering believers together in churches. The Spirit applies your message and I have the Spirit in me from the moment I believed you died for me. I have forgiveness of sins—God's acceptance of my sin-prone nature. I wish and claim this for my household, too. I stand amazed that you, Holy and Just God, would make an arrangement for me to have a standing of being just in your sight. You are just and the Justifier. You have indeed revealed this plan, and it is exclusive—replacing any scheme of man. In the computer games, one tries to knock out the many "bad men" who hinder the player; and in life, Jesus, you "knocked out" the wrath of God so that I would not suffer. I have peace with you, God. But I seem to have a dove and a mad dog inside of me creating great conflict. I wish the mad dog would go away. Thank you, God, for being patient with me. Though I feel inadequate, I know I have such worth in your sight. I will try to give my life regularly in such a way as to show my devotion and use the help of being with other believers in a church. May all of us believers not hide in the church building, but go out to others, be "sent ones," as you intend. Also, I am happy that your love and arrangement in Christ is not just for me but for all people of any ethnic group or language. Thank you, Jesus and Holy Spirit, for interceding for me!

(May you express yourself in prayer using your vocabulary and style.)

LETTERS OF
LOVE

Therefore you do not lack any spiritual gift as you eagerly wait for our Lord Jesus Christ to be revealed. (1 Corinthians 1:7. Chapters 1–2)

PART ONE: No lack of spiritual gifts! What have we read that might be related? Jesus: "I will be with you always, to the very end of the age" (Matthew 28:20). Paul: "The Spirit intercedes for the saints" (Romans 8:27). With all that presence and support, surely we should picture ourselves as led by the hand of God. Besides that, Paul was writing to those in the church at Corinth who had the company and encouragement of other men and women believers. Paul hailed them as standing sanctified (made clean) in God's sight; by Christ Jesus, of course. They may not be entirely holy, in fact, in daily conduct. This twofold life is true of other believers in other cities, and in our city today. Gifts and helps, we have.

PART TWO: Wait for our Lord Jesus Christ. A few saw him leave beyond the clouds. Jesus said people would see him return in the midst of great glory and power. Apparently many will see him return. "Wait" could mean (1) do nothing, or (2) do one thing while anticipating another thing. By the words that follow, it appears Paul means the latter; that we are to work hard on our daily lifestyle while anticipating the return of Christ Jesus. Note three words describing God's part: *keep, called,* and *faithful.* So, in the midst of good things and bad things in this life, we certainly do wish for and anticipate Jesus' return trusting God's strong part.

(Paul wrote from Ephesus after having been at Corinth on a previous journey.)

Don't you know that you yourselves are God's temple and that God's Spirit lives in you? (1 Corinthians 3:16). *Your body is a temple of the Holy Spirit, who is in you, whom you have received from God.* (6:19. Chapters 3–9)

Halloween masks and costumes are always on the outside. The Holy Spirit is IN the believer! Grandma and Granddad come only for a visit, whereas the Spirit lives on in you! We are even called temples. The Jews had used a portable tabernacle in centuries past, and then had an elegant permanent Temple in Jerusalem. However, Paul is not referring to buildings, but to our bodies!

Remember how we referred to Jesus' leaving of this world and the giving of the Holy Spirit in his place, "It is for your good that I am going away. Unless I go away, the Counselor will not come to you; but if I go, I will send him to you" (John 16:7). Jesus limited himself to being in one place at a time, within a human body. Not so the Holy Spirit, for he did not take a body. As Paul here stresses, the Holy Spirit takes your body, my body and the body of each believer! The believer is thereby sacred in God's sight. Thank you.

The Holy Spirit is not some mystical vagueness. He is part (somehow) of the God and of Christ Jesus who created this world and sovereignly oversees it. Jesus said the Spirit will teach us and guide us. Paul stresses the reminder that lives of believers were bought at the cost of the life of Jesus Christ. Hence, a natural response should be to use one's body very carefully as a temple. Awesome!

So, if you think you are standing firm, be careful that you don't fall! (1 Corinthians 10:12. Chapter 10)

Likely each of us should memorize this verse and the one following. A little ego may help you get a job, and more may help you lose it. We warn a child when standing near the edge of a cliff that he may fall. Last year, one in our community fell from a cliff and died. But in moral matters, it seems so difficult to see the edge—until, upon falling, one looks back. Hindsight is....

The advantage of being in a church, or a small group, for accountability is that others can often see more clearly and warn us.

What? There is no new temptation? Drugs and distortions of sex are old; selfishness and anger are not new. Every temptation plagued others before you came along. That's comforting, for you and I have the same problem as others. So, if they have found help, we can, too. God shows boundaries to help stop us from going too far. God will slow us down so that we can make a turn in life and not go over the broken "Bridge of No Return."

May we look at Paul, eye to eye. Are we looking for the way out of temptation, the way to escape? Sometimes you and I don't really want to make the turn and miss the bridge of destruction, for the approach is so beautiful. Paul, the name of each of us belongs on the pages along with those you are scolding in Corinth.

For I received from the Lord what I also passed on to you.... (1 Corinthians 11:23. Chapter 11)

Jesus did not tell us what shape or size to build church buildings. He did not tell us to set crosses or fish symbols in our homes. Paul records how Jesus wants to be remembered—with a meal, sort of. It is not a meal for sustaining the body, nor a time of merriment. It is a time of imitating the last supper Jesus had with his disciples.

Common bread was used to symbolize his body. His body was broken, crucified with the purpose of benefiting you and me. The common drink of the day was used to symbolize his blood. In this double way, Jesus stressed that his life was completely given. Jesus had called himself the "Bread of Heaven," and with trembling was willing to drink the cup symbolizing the wrath of God. Hence, believers today are to reenact this in remembrance until he returns. (Scholarly people debate the extent of the presence of Christ in this event.)

May we liken our lives to the clothes on the clothesline. Remember the old fashioned kind: a post in one corner of the yard, the other post over yonder. One post stands for the first time Christ came; the other post for the future return of Christ. The clothes on the line represent our lives inbetween. Perhaps we're close to the "return" post.

This position in time is humbling, for it was at the cost of the life of the Son. It is encouraging, for we have fellowship with others who have the same needs. It is exhilarating, for it reminds us that Jesus' words will not fail. He will return.

What's next, Lord?

But eagerly desire the greater gifts... (1 Corinthians 12:31). *These three remain: faith, hope and love. But the greatest of these is love.* (13:13. Chapters 12–14)

The Spirit works in our (the believers') lives by facilitating various gifts (12:4). In the midst of such variety, there is but one unifying purpose: "The common good" (12:7). Paul is not talking about handcrafting skills, nor mental agility, but about new characteristics in our lives by means of the Holy Spirit. What these are is even determined by the Spirit, as a master teacher intimately knows each pupil (12:11).

Consider the body. It has many parts and no part can boast over any other part—obviously. Parts do not merge but remain their distinct selves and, if one part suffers, other parts are affected—obviously. Well, "You are the body of Christ, and each one of you is a part of it" (12:27). Now that, too, is obvious.

Each of us needs to learn which particular gifts the Spirit has given, but every one of us is to work on LOVE. In fact, Christ put the matter as a command, "My command is this: Love each other as I have loved you" (John 15:12). He even said that others will be surprised at your love.

"All men will know that you are my disciples if you love one another" (John 13:35). So much responsibility is placed on us, such as even loving one's enemies and neighbors (Matthew 5:44, 19:19, 22:39). Is that why love is greater than faith and hope, because of the depth of responsibility placed upon us? Help!

For what I received I passed on to you as of first importance: that Christ died for our sins according to the Scriptures, that he was buried, that he was raised on the third day according to the Scriptures. (1 Corinthians 15:3–4. Chapter 15)

Did you ever read a book and then wonder if the author said anything new? Paul summarizes here near the end of his epistle. We do have a distinctively new message, making life exhilarating.

Let's list Paul's expressions: (1) It is this gospel, good news, whereby one is saved. (2) Christ died for your sins, and my sins. (3) That death was according to God's plan as announced in the Scriptures (Old Testament). (4) Christ was buried (the certainty that he died). (5) Christ came back from death (from among the dead ones) on the third day, the very schedule Christ announced beforehand, to be alive. (6) This, too, was according to the Scriptures. (7) He appeared to many people as hard evidence. (8) His resurrection is evidence of the resurrection for us. (9) Anyone who says Christ was not raised, is still under the guilt of his sins. (10) Christ is the first of all who will rise. (11) Believers who have died are likened to have fallen asleep. (12) At the resurrection, each believer will be given a new body, far superior to the present one.

If physical death is likened to being asleep, then what is the next occasion of being awake? The Resurrection! Let's jump and shout!

Death has been swallowed up in victory. (1 Corinthians 15:54. Chapters 15–16)

Victory will be evident in the new body to be given, for it is certainly not evident in the old flesh-and-blood one we have now. Look again at Paul's words describing that new body: imperishable, glory, power, spiritual. Since we can comprehend that this earthly body is appropriate for the now-time, why can't we grasp that there will be a new kind of body for the future-time?

I love Paul's taunt as he uses Hosea 13:14: "Where, O death, is your victory? Where, O death, is your sting?"

When I read these words at a funeral service, I read with sarcastic laughter; for Paul is laughing in Death's face. Can you laugh with joy? Immediately, Paul turns serious, as though reading a legal document—a will, God's will. "The sting [fear] of death is sin [the result of sin]....The power of sin is the law." The stranglehold of sin is defined and heralded to us by law. Then, in spite of what we suppose we will receive, the final statement in the will regarding distribution of benefits from God to us is, "But thanks be to God! He gives us the victory through our Lord Jesus Christ."

Jump!

Shout....

Sing....

Cry!

Hallelujah!

And he has committed to us the message of reconcilia-tion. We are therefore Christ's ambassadors....(2 Corinthians 5:19–20)

Christ hands every believer an assignment. From then on, we have two lives: One life is the care of this earthly body, while the other life is the anticipation of the heavenly body. As one goes to the store to buy a new dress or suit, one smiles with visions of the choices to be made using the credit card to guarantee the purchase. Similarly, the conviction in one's heart by the Holy Spirit is the guarantee of the new attire to be given by God. True, we must pay for credit cards; but Jesus has already paid for our new life. We desire that new attire, new life, with the Lord; but must be content with the earthly attire we have for now.

Our assignment now is to live, striving to please God. Our new compulsion and excitement in life is so strong that Paul declares we are new persons. Much of the previous selfish goals and idols of life are replaced by very new and different reasons for being.

God does not send angel messengers, but gives to us the message of reconciliation. We have an assignment to touch the lives of others, letting this new inner compulsion invite others to accept what we have found. We implore others to accept the righteousness of God made clear by Jesus Christ. We have a new responsibility of being ambassadors! He trusted the disciples then; he trusts us now.

But the fruit of the Spirit is love, joy, peace, patience, kindness, goodness, faithfulness, gentleness and self-control. Against such there is no law. (Galatians 5:22–23)

Paul writes with such clarity, with such vigor, in presenting the standing the believer has in Christ. Shades of his Epistle to the Romans!

However, we are not the cheerleaders at the side of the playing field but are the players on the field. Strangely, we are playing in both directions, for we have a sinful nature striving to go one direction and a new spirit-led nature striving in opposition. Let's pause as we read the goals of the sinful nature: "Sexual immorality, impurity and debauchery; idolatry and witchcraft; hatred, discord, jealousy, fits of rage, selfish ambition,…and the like."

Now, note the goals for the Spirit-led nature: "Love, joy, peace, patience, kindness, goodness, faithfulness, gentleness and self-control." Indeed, they are in the opposite direction. These are accomplished by living among Christian people, rather than as a hermit. Do you love people outside your family? Do you have joy and peace to the extent that it is conspicuous to others such as those at work? How is your patience, kindness and goodness toward your neighbors? Do others observe and comment upon your faithfulness and self-control? No law prohibits living in these ways.

Maybe, I'm afraid to ask, "What else?"

His incomparably great power for us who believe.
(Ephesians 1:19a)

POWER. That word occurs eight times in this epistle. We also translate that Greek word into our daily vocabulary as "dynamite."

Paul wants us to realize this power working in our lives is "like the working of his mighty strength, which he exerted in Christ when he raised him from the dead...." Now that's high octane! Paul wants every believer to have power from the love Christ exerts (3:17–19). May our lives be filled, ready for the daily living where the rubber meets the road.

Paul propels us beyond our human comprehension "according to his [God's] power that is at work within us" (3:20). Finally, he indicates how to have God's power: "Put on the full armor of God: truth, righteousness, peace, faith, salvation, word of God [Scriptures], and prayer" (6:10ff).

On the one hand, God gives power from Christ; while, on the other hand, God expects us to use responsible conduct that will keep God's power in our lives. The roller coaster at the fairgrounds imparts the power to put us up and down, left and right. Yet, we are safe if we stay in our seats. Likewise, we are safe as we trust the Spirit to lead us through the ups and downs of daily living as long as we stay in our seats—keeping the armor on us. Now we understand the power which Christ promised (Acts 1:8). This is power not offered by other religions!

Rejoice in the Lord always. I will say it again: Rejoice! (Philippians 4:4)

"Rejoice, rejoice, oh Christian,
Lift up your voice and sing,
Eternal hallelujahs,
To Jesus Christ the King!"

In such fashion, many hymns encourage joy and rejoicing. This is a distinction of the body of believers. They have reason to sing when together corporately, and just as much in the privacy of daily living.

Now wait, isn't this verse rather naive? No, for Paul had experienced adversity. In the midst of all Paul was saying to the church at Philippi, and in the midst of all the systematic theology he wrote to believers at Rome, he says this more as a summary. It is like a volcanic explosion after all the warmth down inside has had time to accumulate.

But how do we apply this? Turn to this after each hurt in life; after the death of a loved one; after the loss of a job; after being wronged by neighbor or friend; after observing so many wrongs presented by the news media; after admitting that you, yourself, are so far from being perfect. Really, this is a prescription for daily living. If we are in the habit of rejoicing when not hurt, it will be easier to rejoice when hurt.

"Rejoice in the Lord,...again...."

When Christ, who is your life, appears, then you also will appear with him in glory. (Colossians 3:4)

We may not be good enough actors to be given the principal part, but we would like at least to appear on stage with the principal. We understand that we would like to have our names mentioned in the reviews along with, of course, the hero and heroine. When Jesus Christ appears (returns to earth), you and I, and other believers, will appear "on stage" with Him! There will be great fanfare, properly called "glory."

How did Paul a few sentences earlier describe the change in status for the believer? "But now he has reconciled you by Christ's physical body through death to present you holy in his sight, without blemish and free from accusation..." (1:22). Only because of Christ do we have a right to associate with him. We shall appear with him!

Responsibility goes with privilege. Reread 1:10–12 and 23. We must live carefully in order to give some semblance of worthiness, even though we'll never in this life be perfect. We need to grow in the knowledge of God in order to know how to please him. Incidentally, isn't this true in the husband-wife relationship—the need to communicate and know each other in order to please? Responsibility is continued in Chapter 3 with specific recommendations for your lifelong "job description."

You shall appear with Christ! What's next, Lord?

Asleep…asleep…asleep. (1 Thessalonians 4:13–18)

Ignorant? We understand in general, although not in detail. We have a hope which is certainly based upon facts from history. Jesus lived, died and rose again. That all happened as announced in Scriptures written centuries in advance of it happening. Jesus said several times that he would leave and return. Even the religious leaders understood that Jesus meant what he said.

Paul elaborates saying that people will be brought with Jesus. Who? Those who have died, having faith in Jesus Christ. These are called "asleep." Furthermore, Christ will return accompanied by much fanfare of God's making, not man's.

There will be two grand movements of people. The first: those believers who have died ("dead in Christ"). Then: those still bodily alive. Both groups will meet the Lord Jesus Christ in space and remain with him!

That, indeed, is encouragement in spite of planning to file bankruptcy, in spite of learning cancer has spread in your body, in spite of receiving a phone call that your dear relative has committed suicide. (Suicide does not change one's eternal destiny.)

Whatever the reason for death, everyone who believes in Christ and dies is called "asleep." The asleep ones will rise first, and whoever is alive at the time of his return will tag along in the second group. Beautiful—after being asleep, we will awake to meet Christ!

The one who holds it back will continue to do so....(2 Thessalonians 2:7)

We trust dams; but when one breaks, there is loss of life, vegetation and soil. The beaver trusts his dam to hold back enough water to store his food and maintain his lodge. If the dam breaks completely, the habitat will be lost.

God is in the dam business. He is holding back rebellion, holding back one dedicated to lawlessness...the one who exalts himself to the extent of pronouncing himself to be god—Satan.

The holding is only until a proper time. God chooses the time for his major events, for no one can hurry him. We often wonder why God waits so long for his events.

Jesus will overthrow this evil one. There will not be any equality in the match, simply no contest. Jesus will overthrow by speaking. That should not be a surprise. For when Jesus was on earth, he simply spoke to evil spirits and they obeyed.

The sad part is that some people will fall for the evil one's work of counterfeiting God's work. In the meantime, God holds back—keeps in check—lawless work in this world. This holding seems to be by the Holy Spirit. It is difficult to imagine what this life would be without this restraint. Thanks be to God, the dam holds!

God our Savior, who wants all men to be saved. (1 Timothy 2:3–4)

We want all our loved ones to be saved from disease. Some are and some are not. God wants all to be saved for eternal life. Some are and some are not.

Why is that? If God can influence Satan, why can't he influence every one of us in our choices? He could, but he chooses not to force us, not to make us robots. Herein lies a mystery which is the meeting of God's sovereignty with man's responsibility. You and I cannot understand the blending of these two. Did you ever watch the water of a river enter a bay? Watch day after day and observe the river water in one location one day and in a very different place another day. Even then, we don't see what mixing is taking place under the surface. We can only describe the event on the surface, and that's very superficial. So, also, with God and man.

The testimony about God has been given, as Paul says, by the one Mediator, Christ Jesus. Jesus said of himself, "No one comes to the Father except through me" (John 14:6). Paul already said that we believers have been given the message of reconciliation and that we are to implore others to come and accept. (2 Corinthians 5) We, too, are to have a deep desire that all be saved. Yet, in practicality, we can only extend ourselves to a few specific people. God uses us within his desire that all be saved for eternal life.

Here am I, use me.

While we wait for the blessed hope—the glorious appearing of our great God and Savior, Jesus Christ.... (Titus 2:13)

What do you do while you wait for the road construction crew to allow you to drive on? You may look at your appointment book, may make a cellular call, may pray for a friend in crisis, some may inwardly curse and swear. Christians are waiting for the return of Christ. We don't know for how long.

While we wait, we are to live very carefully. That includes saying "no" to "ungodliness and worldly passions, and to live self-controlled, upright and godly lives in this present age, while we wait..." (2:12). A youngster could be careless in the excitement of running to the store, and drop the money through the sewer grate. The Christian must not be careless, but be diligent in conduct at all times while waiting.

We're waiting for the return of Jesus Christ who is our Savior and our God. During the first years of the Christian church, the resurrection of Jesus was stressed (in the book of Acts). During the succeeding generations of the church, the return of Christ was stressed. Still, the Christian message is distinct from other religions by the certainty of the return of the Savior. Our Savior, upon his return, would like to find believers having some measure of success at living in a way pleasing to him. Paul gives some specific suggestions. Live carefully while waiting for Christ.

How shall we escape if we ignore such a great salvation? (Hebrews 2:3. Chapters 1–2)

Sometimes teachers ask questions for which the answer is so obvious that the class knows, and the answer need not be stated. So, also, here. Is there any other possible plan to escape the consequence of our sinful nature if one rejects God's plan? No, obviously.

PART A: Sin is any failure to obey God. God does not forget or ignore our sin. Sin does not belong close to the holiness of God. He is righteous and must judge sin. Deep down inside ourselves we even expect judgment. God provided One to take our judgment upon himself.

PART B: God's plan of salvation was sketched here and there throughout the Old Testament. Police artists work and work to sketch a composite of the face of the one they want to find. The four Gospels show that Jesus Christ matches the composite of the one sketched in the Old Testament—our Savior. Those who walked and talked with Jesus confirmed his character as being more than man, even God. There was no inconsistency found in him.

PART C: The Holy Spirit came upon Jews and Gentiles, not starting a new message, but applying the message about Jesus. Even in the midst of persecution, as recorded in history, a most notable characteristic is the change in the lives of believers.

PART D: Corollary to all the above: How does my life and your life show that we cling to this salvation, and that our lifestyle is changed within the family and workplace?

Let us then approach the throne of grace with confidence, so that we may receive mercy and find grace to help us in our time of need. (Hebrews 4:16. Chapters 3–6)

This paragraph starts with the word "therefore," as do several others in this epistle. Therefore—a consequence or conclusion to what has already been written. As a consequence or conclusion to Jesus Christ being our great high priest, we hold firmly to all that is our faith.

Has the teenager remembered the combination to his lock on the locker at school, or has he perhaps transposed the numbers? Does he or she have confidence to unlock and enter? Every Christian has confidence to approach God because Jesus unlocked and opened the door of access.

It would be in our best interest to want what God wants us to have. One time, I invited a lady friend out to dinner. She presumed we'd go to an inexpensive restaurant and dressed accordingly. I planned and did take her to quite a nice one; I wanted her to want the niceness that I intended. (The illustration breaks down, for I should have told her where we were going.) God does make clear to us that he wants us to have eternal life; that's where he wants us to go.

In the meantime, we have confidence we'll find "mercy and find grace to help us in our time of need."

So Christ was sacrificed once to take away the sins of many people; and he will appear a second time, not to bear sin, but to bring salvation to those who are waiting for him. (Hebrews 9:28. Chapters 7–10)

As you leave the store and pay for the items at the cashier, do you expect to be stopped in the parking lot and told to pay a second time? No. So, Christ paid with his life once for our sins, hence, he does not need to pay again. Likewise, if your friend pays for a dinner, you cannot step forward to pay for the same meal. Neither can you step forward and offer to pay for your sins; for Christ already did so, completely. That is the very purpose for which he came to earth centuries ago.

When he returns, it will be for a different purpose. When the professor continues the lecture after lunch, he likely speaks on another aspect than he did in the morning. Jesus finished with the problem of our sin—he has already substituted for us and satisfied Holy God. What topic will Jesus have in mind next time? Completion of salvation. Now we own salvation, but it is not "in hand." Jesus will bring salvation to his believers. More correctly, Jesus will have us enter salvation when he calls us as his believers to rise and meet him.

And what more?

Now faith is being sure of what we hope for and certain of what we do not see. (Hebrews 11:1. Chapter 11)

God, the Holy Spirit, guided the prophets of old to write of things in the future, many of which did not take place in their lifetime. There was also the period, about four hundred years, after the last writing of the prophets when there was no more revealing from God. Yet, people were expected to have hope.

There are two opposite types of hope. In one case, an ill person is in the hospital with cancer in much of the body; then, also, pneumonia begins. The loved ones hope the ill one will soon come home to lead a normal life. They hope that because of their love. But, it is not realistic hope, for it is contrary to the direction the facts strongly suggest. We should call that wishful thinking.

The other hope is based upon many factors all pointing in the direction of the hope. I buy tickets to visit grandchildren across the country. I have been in good health. Then, the grandchildren have hope in my visit based upon reliable facts. The Christian hope is based upon all the promises that raised the hopes of the Old Testament people. Those promises that centered upon the first coming of the Savior have taken place. Other promises pertaining to the future were explained by Jesus. Now we have his word, God's Word, for these things.

Simply said, we are certain of what we do not yet see!

Therefore, since we are surrounded by such a great cloud of witnesses, let us throw off everything that hinders and the sin that so easily entangles, and let us run with perseverance the race marked out for us. (Hebrews 12:1. Chapters 12–13)

The team is excited about playing on the home court! Is the court, itself, better? No, but there will be thousands of people of that town cheering for their team. It is a very real psychological advantage to play on the home court surrounded by a cloud of friendly witnesses.

We believers are surrounded by many like-minded people in our worship service. At communion, especially on World Communion Sunday, we think of the multitude of other believers scattered about the world; they speak other languages and use other customs.

Lift your sight. A great cloud of people have lived as witnesses and have died. Think of them as in the air watching. How many can you name? Reread Chapter 11 and add those you can name. Do you have a vision of a cloud of witnesses?

We Christians are always on the home court with these countless ones cheering us on. We're in a race with an end— eternal life. A race also implies the endeavor of trying to stay ahead of others. Our case is not to be better than, ahead of, other Christians, but to stay ahead of the temptations of Satan.

Get set...go!

If any of you lacks wisdom, he should ask God, who gives generously to all without finding fault, and it will be given to him. (James 1:5)

You and I as adults can admit we have not "arrived," for we lack wisdom so frequently. There still needs to be change in our lives, "Perseverance must finish its work so that you may be mature and complete..." (1:4).

Sometimes the youngster is fearful of asking his teacher a question. The teacher may seem cross that day or so busy. Strange, also, that often Christians are fearful of asking God for wisdom. "It is such a small matter....My problem is so insignificant compared with what is happening to people in other parts of the world." But, ASK.

Quite astounding is that God will not find fault in our asking. The teacher may sternly retort, "I wrote that assignment on the board, yesterday." God will not reprove our asking. Although God has told us over and over his general directions for living, he will not reprove us for asking about our daily lives. He reserves, of course, the choice of how to answer the request.

"It will be given." This a strong affirmation along with the recommendation not to doubt. The kayaker must approach the wave in a certain way, for if he dallies or doubts the technique available, he will be tossed. Ask God!

Praise be to the God and Father of our Lord Jesus Christ! In his great mercy he has given us new birth into a living hope through the resurrection of Jesus Christ from the dead, and into an inheritance that can never perish, spoil or fade— kept in heaven for you, who through faith are shielded by God's power until the coming of the salvation that is ready to be revealed in the last time. In this you greatly rejoice, though now for a little while you may have had to suffer grief in all kinds of trials. These have come so that your faith—of greater worth than gold, which perishes even though refined by fire—may be proved genuine and may result in praise, glory and honor when Jesus Christ is revealed. Though you have not seen him, you love him; and even though you do not see him now, you believe in him and are filled with an inexpressible and glorious joy, for you are receiving the goal of your faith, the salvation of your souls. (1 Peter 1:3–9)

Why try to add anything to this? Put this on your refrigerator or in the car to read daily.

Stand back and shout, "Hallelujah!"

Through these he has given us his very great and precious promises, so that through them you may participate in the divine nature and escape the corruption in the world caused by evil desires....And you will receive a rich welcome into the eternal kingdom of our Lord and Savior Jesus Christ. (2 Peter 1:4, 11)

"Well, good morning, John and Jane. Come in. It's so good to have you." It will be a much more grand welcome from our Lord! We suppose it will be in the midst of all the glory surrounding Christ. He will call us by name and angels will undoubtedly rejoice again (Luke 15:7–10). We won't look around at the "furnishings," for all eyes and emotions will be centered upon our Savior and our God.

God's promises guide us and even afford protection from corruption as we live daily. Each of us can admit that as we overcome one difficulty, there often seems to be two new ones. Since God is not yet overthrowing Satan, we can be confident that corruption in the world will continue. We cannot sit back and complain about all the corruption around us. Peter is stressing that we use God's power to avoid corruption in our lives. He mentions this again, later. (2:20)

After working hard upon our own lives, we look forward to the final escape and that rich welcome!

Dear friends, now we are children of God, and what we will be has not yet been made known. But we know that when he appears, we shall be like him, for we shall see him as he is. (1 John 3:2)

"You should meet him when he's not at a party. My, he's different in his own home. You wouldn't admire him if you lived with him day after day." We do know Jesus well enough to admire and to worship him. We also know there is indeed much more to his character he could not show us while at the "party" here on earth. But, we have no trepidation. We know we shall be pleased when we see Jesus in his full Godliness.

Even more amazing, we shall have some likeness to him! We shall be given a new body that cannot sin; that certainly is a likeness to Jesus. We suppose that we won't have any consciousness of having been "red or yellow, black or white" here on earth, but simply that we be like Jesus. The smaller embers in the fireplace glow afresh when pushed close to the large embers, and then brilliant colors spread across all the embers. Likewise, the brilliance of Jesus will engulf us.

In the meantime, back on the ranch—earth, that is, "Everyone who has this hope in him purifies himself, just as he is pure" (3:3). "No one who lives in him keeps on sinning" (3:6). John continues with this stress upon our daily effort. We cannot simply stand back and smile at the sunshine and the rain, but must repeatedly put the hoe to the crop.

To him who is able to keep you from falling and to present you before his glorious presence without fault and with great joy—to the only God our Savior be glory, majesty, power and authority, through Jesus Christ our Lord, before all ages, now and forevermore! Amen. (Jude 24–25)

I have not climbed a glacial mountain, but I understand that each climber is roped to the others. Thus, when one slips, the others break the fall and give time for that one to regain proper position. Jesus intends to keep you from falling. Again, there is an incomprehensible mixing of God's sovereignty and man's responsibility. Jude began his Epistle with the same thought: "Kept by Jesus Christ."

Even better than being helped to plant both feet on the top of the mountain, we will be lifted into the presence of our God! We will be declared to be without fault. Remember, Jesus took our place for judgment of our sin, and we are acquitted. The youngster runs with joy into the arms of Grandma, but each believer will have far greater joy in meeting God.

Can we sing? Well, try singing verse 25. Try in the bathroom or in the car by yourself. Praise God, sing to God. Make up your own tune. Sing at the stoplight. Amen! Amen!

CONVERSATIONAL PRAYER

Now we have read the many epistles and letters from 1 Corinthians through Jude. Surely there are many matters to highlight in prayer.

Dear Father, Son and Holy Spirit, you have provided so much for me, being present with me, even calling me a temple. You keep me focused by means of the communion table where I am reminded that you, Jesus, gave your life for me; and I certainly do have faith and hope. My love seems to have its ups and downs, but your love doesn't falter. Jesus, you came back from among the dead to give me confidence in the resurrection of myself sometime in the future. "Faith is the victory!...O glorious victory, That overcomes the world." Yea, and I have a new title of ambassador, whether I am a plumber or politician. Help me with the gracefulness to tell others; and I'll keep working on my own character, trying to show love, joy and peace. I won't be put in jail for that. You lead me with a power and confidence so that I'm ready to live, or to "sleep," knowing of the awakening with you. Thanks, also, for the cloud of witnesses "rooting" for me until that final salvation. Thank you, Jesus, for wanting me to come into your presence. I'll even have some likeness to yourself.

Thank you, thank you.

(Say something, sing something, let something burst out in your own words!)

YET TO COME

Look, he is coming with the clouds, and every eye will see him, even those who pierced him; and all the peoples of the earth will mourn because of him. So shall it be! Amen. (Revelation 1:7)

Act II, Scene III: The Future

He is coming—not the ruler of a country—HE is coming. Christians have been watching for centuries, but that does not detract from the certainty of his coming. Jesus said so. John, by a vision, saw Jesus return as though it were happening right before his eyes.

"Every eye will see him." At a royal party, a trumpet will sound—evidently to get the attention of everyone and to silence the guests. Then the royal person will be clearly announced by name and credentials. Everyone in the great hall will see that person. Upon heralding Jesus, every person on the whole earth will see his coming. No one will fail to see him, even those who have died this death, even those who participated in the Crucifixion.

All people seeing him will mourn. It seems that nonbelievers will mourn because they failed to acknowledge Jesus as God. Believers at the scene will mourn as they acknowledge that they were the reason for Jesus' suffering.

This return of Jesus is given at the beginning of this epistle as an assurance while one reads of all the coming disasters. It shows that Christ has control, his accomplishments cannot be thwarted by man. He will come.

What will happen when he comes?

The city does not need the sun or the moon to shine on it, for the glory of God gives it light, and the Lamb is its lamp. (Revelation 21:23. Vs.22–27)

The visions gave John many gruesome events to record. We will be glad if we do not need to live through any of them.

Finally, in contrast, John is shown pleasant things: a new heaven, a new kind of earth and a new Jerusalem. But there is no temple to "house" God, for God himself is there. There is no sun or moon. God is given as two persons; the second being the Lamb, Jesus Christ. The Lamb is central in the sequences portrayed, being mentioned over two dozen times in this letter. God and the Lamb are the light for the people.

Somehow there will be the functioning of nations, for they will acknowledge God and bring proper tribute. The people who will be there are those whose names are in the Lamb's book of life (vs.27). All other people have already been cast aside (20:15).

Believers are promised wonderful things. In this case, there is not much explanation given. May we be content that the arrangement will be the best and, therefore, simply amazing and glorious to us. Only God can put these things in place.

Anything else?

I warn everyone who hears the words of the prophecy of this book; if anyone adds anything to them, God will add to him the plagues described in this book. And if anyone takes words away from this book of prophecy, God will take away from him his share in the tree of life and in the holy city, which are described in this book. (Revelation 22:18–19)

John wrote this book nearly a half-century after the other parts of the Canon, so it seems fitting that it be placed last in the Bible. This book tells of things yet to come; so again, it is fitting to be last.

In simple words, no one has authority to change the message of this book by adding to or subtracting from it. After all, John did not make up a story but passed on what God's angel showed him and told him to write. One who changes this message will not receive the very goal being offered and described as so desirable—the holy city. And such a person will not go unnoticed but will experience now, in this life, various disasters herein described.

Most believers understand that God, the Holy Spirit, carefully directed people in writing these booklets now put together as the Bible (2 Peter 1:21. For further reading, look for the subject of Inspiration of the Bible). Since this warning occurs on the last page of the Bible, many believe this is an awesome warning regarding the Bible as a whole.

If we trust John to be honest in presenting the multitude of visions, then we must trust him in his honesty of presenting this warning.

How do you end, John?

Amen. Come, Lord Jesus. The grace of the Lord Jesus be with God's people. Amen. (Revelation 22:20–21)

A daughter might say to her mother and father who visited from a far away place, "Your visit has seemed so short. You have been so supportive of me. Please come again soon."

Yes, Jesus' visit on this earth was rather short, yet long enough to show us God's supportive love; short, but long enough to show us how to please God. When Jesus visits again, he will usher us into his presence for a long time—forever!

Can you anticipate his return with excitement, with exhilaration? Do you wish it today, tomorrow, whether you are in the midst of ease or difficulty?

Amen.

    Come,

        Lord Jesus!

           .... (your name)

CONVERSATIONAL PRAYER

We have read the last book of the Bible, Revelation. It certainly is fitting to be placed last. What comes to mind for this last prayer will vary considerably from person to person.

Our Father in Heaven, somehow you came to earth and clearly showed us your plan of salvation. You gave us riches by Christ's life. I shake my head in awe and wonder. Although, on the one hand, you left earth; yet on the other hand, you have remained in us. You are a good "supervisor," giving us tools for our earthly assignment of carrying the message of reconciliation. I almost fear your return as that will entail so much judgment and disaster over the entire earth. However, you have told us enough so that we may look beyond to the glory surrounding Christ's return. You have shown your holiness and your love. With my vivid imagination, I've often wondered if you established life on other planets. If you have, I trust that you have loved those in a way fitting your holiness. Again, my imagination has difficulty with the thought of eternity, yet I am confident I'll be happy once I have entered. Often, while hiking on the mountains or kayaking on the sound [Puget Sound], I've sung, "O Lord, my God/ when I, in awesome wonder,/ Consider all the worlds Thy hands have made./ Then sings my soul,/ my Savior God, to Thee:/ How great Thou art./ How great Thou art!…" I will continue trying to be consistent in loving you with my heart, soul and mind. As I rejoice in you, I look forward to the Day: "For all the saints who from their labors rest…." Gladly, and only in Jesus' name, I pray.

(Are you praying, singing, shouting, or all of the above?)

EPILOGUE

In a Mustard Seed

There is NO message comparable to this one that centers in Jesus Christ! Let's consider the message in a nut shell.

This is a revelation. God intervened many times and in many ways to direct certain people. God revealed his plan, step by step. So many generations and even centuries were involved that the people must often have wondered what would be next, and when. Much of this has already become history by our time, yet even more significant matters lie ahead of us. It is not what man would have made up himself.

This message has a writing, the Bible. Suppose that the USA Congress voted unanimously (that would be amazing in itself) to have 40-plus people selected to write 66 booklets over the next 1,500 years, and then all 66 booklets were to be bound in one volume and taken to all the world as a new religion. What chance would there be of any continuity of message? What chance that events foretold would take place, sometimes centuries later? What chance of this new message truly being the message that the God of creation wanted for us? Who would live long enough to choose the 40-plus writers? We find that the Holy Spirit was the "committee of one" to choose those writers, guide as to what was written, and providentially protect in the preservation of those writings. Many portions of its history have been verified by various branches of our sciences. We have confidence that predictions yet in the future will indeed take place in due time.

This message reveals a Trinity. Somehow God is one

and also, at the same time and always, three Persons—Father, Son and Holy Spirit. How can God divide himself? I cannot explain this. I can and will rely on the Trinity.

A number of other questions raised in this text are not answered. Some are answered well by scholarly writers using many pages; others remain a mystery. For example, the relationship of God working in a sovereign way, and yet expecting responsibility of us.

This message says there is a battle. Two enormous powers—God and Satan—are in a struggle for the allegiance of man and woman. God is in control, and yet allows (strangely to our minds) Satan considerable latitude of operation, but only for this age. It was with Satan's assistance that man has come to have a sin-prone nature. God's plan is to overcome that sinful nature and, thus, in the end, beat Satan in his power struggle and also to defeat Satan himself.

This message presents a problem. It is like a fatal disease. It is called sin. "Sin is any want [lack] of conformity unto, or transgression of, the law of God" (Westminster Shorter Catechism, Number 14). The Psalmist had a clear perspective, "If you, O Lord, kept a record of sins; O Lord, who could stand?" (Psalm 130:3).

This message warns of two destinies. One is very desirable, being in God's presence; the other is utterly undesirable and the lingering regret is implied by Paul, "With everlasting destruction and shut out from the presence of the Lord and from the majesty of his power..." (2 Thessalonians 1:9).

This message has a Savior. All mankind wants some form of savior. This Savior, Jesus Christ, really walked on this earth. There is so much testimony by his followers and so much vehement opposition by his detractors that the world agrees Jesus was really here for a few years. He was, in many ways, certified as sent by the God who created this world and mankind, and frequently intervenes in this world. This Jesus Christ showed himself to be God. Then he died willingly and with a purpose, as if he were an animal sacrifice—a ransom, a payment—for our atonement (at-one-ment) with God. But he was Victor over death, which becomes an attestation of the approval of God the Father. The Savior, then, is this special person, not some special few of us men and women making ourselves so good that we are of ourselves acceptable by Holy God.

This message lays an urgent responsibility upon the conduct of each believer whose lifestyle often will become different in many ways from that found in the rest of society. Admittedly, believers do not agree on the levels of importance of various manners of conduct. Yet, the believer cannot be a mere observer.

This message has a commission. Each believer is to tell other people and hence use the opportunity at home, work, school or play. Some believers may move to a foreign land to share the message. We also need to be able to receive a believer FROM a foreign land.

This message has rewards of enormous consequences: forgiveness, peace, joy, purpose, love, patience, self-control and other qualities in this life. And, to come: ETERNAL LIFE!

Have YOU accepted this Person? If so, then God accepts you into his kingdom and there is joy in heaven. These believers have more joy than followers of other religions, judging by the vast quantity of hymns and music based upon the gospel message. Included in the faith is the return of Jesus Christ and the taking of us to be with God. God wants us with him for a day?...a year?...forever? FOREVER, YES!!

This message has exploded from a seed to become a sprawling tree, otherwise called a kingdom. It knows no bounds of man's national or racial lines. It has moved from one small place on this earth, and from a handful of people, to touching the lives of millions—maybe half the global population around the world!

GUIDE TO READING THROUGH THE BIBLE

Here is the honey; here is the apple—the Bible. Read it in a year's time. Don't wait for January; start today! If you want to start with the New Testament, use October–December.

January	Genesis, Exodus
February	Leviticus, Numbers, Deuteronomy 1-17
March	Deuteronomy 18 to end, Joshua, Judges, Ruth, 1 Samuel
April	2 Samuel, 1 Kings, 2 Kings, 1 Chronicles 1–9
May	1 Chronicles 10 to end, 2 Chronicles, Ezra, Nehemiah, Esther, Job 1–27
June	Job 28 to end, Psalms
July	Proverbs, Ecclesiastes, Song of Solomon, Isaiah
August	Jeremiah, Lamentations, Ezekiel 1–21
September	Ezekiel 22 to end, Daniel, 12 Minor Prophets

October	Matthew, Mark, Luke
November	John, Acts, Romans
December	20 Epistles, Revelation

THE AUTHOR

While working as an electrical engineer for the General Electric Company, friends encouraged him to consider entering the ministry. He prayed about that. In 1953, he graduated from Fuller Theological Seminary and then studied one year at Presbyterian College (a seminary) in Montreal.

He pastored Presbyterian churches in upstate and central New York, and then moved to First Presbyterian Church in Tacoma, Washington. There he served as associate pastor for 22 years. After retirement came an exciting ministry of serving the small Church of the Indian Fellowship in Tacoma.

Martin Ives was born in Seattle, Washington, and attended public school in Seattle and Everett. He accepted Christ as Savior shortly before graduating from the University of Washington in electrical engineering. Then he served briefly as an officer in the U.S. Navy at the end of World War II and continued in the naval reserve as a chaplain.

Lois Brown and Martin were married in 1953 and had four sons and two daughters, all continuing in the faith. Lois died of cancer in 1989. The many grandchildren are a delight.

Martin has been a student of the Bible and their original languages in preparing sermons. Twice he has had the privilege to walk where Jesus walked. In this material, he hopes to propel us back to those announcements God and Jesus made along the history of the Hebrew and Christian centuries. He hopes you'll say, "If only I could have been there then!" And, "I'm coming, Jesus!"

For additional copies of

WHAT'S NEXT, LORD?

have your credit card ready and call

1 (800) 917-BOOK

www.winepresspub.com

or send $11.95 + $1.50 shipping and handling to

WinePress Publishing
PO Box 1406
Mukilteo, WA 98275